Creating a Spiritual Retirement

Creating a Spiritual Retirement

A Guide to the Unseen Possibilities in Our Lives

Molly Srode

Walking Together, Finding the Way
SKYLIGHT PATHS Publishing
Woodstock, Vermont

Creating a Spiritual Retirement:
A Guide to the Unseen Possibilities in Our Lives

Library of Congress Cataloging-in-Publication Data
Srode, Molly, 1937–
Creating a spiritual retirement : a guide to the unseen possibilities in our lives / Molly Srode.
  p. cm.
ISBN 1-893361-75-6 (HC)
1. Spiritual life. 2. Aged—Religious life. 3. Retirees—Religious life. I. Title.
BL625.4 .S69 2003
291.4'4'0846—dc21

2002015993

10   9   8   7   6   5   4   3   2   1

SkyLight Paths Publishing is creating a place where people of different spiritual traditions come together for challenge and inspiration, a place where we can help each other understand the mystery that lies at the heart of our existence.

SkyLight Paths sees both believers and seekers as a community that increasingly transcends traditional boundaries of religion and denomination—people wanting to learn from each other, *walking together, finding the way.*

Manufactured in the United States of America

SkyLight Paths, "Walking Together, Finding the Way" and colophon are trademarks of LongHill Partners, Inc., registered in the U.S. Patent and Trademark Office.

Walking Together, Finding the Way
Published by SkyLight Paths Publishing
A Division of LongHill Partners, Inc.
Sunset Farm Offices, Route 4, P.O. Box 237
Woodstock, VT 05091
Tel: (802) 457-4000   Fax: (802) 457-4004
www.skylightpaths.com

To my husband, Bernie
with love

CONTENTS

Part Three   Practical Spirituality

ACKNOWLEDGMENTS

No book is written alone. Every person who has touched my life has had a part in the writing of this book. I am deeply grateful to each one. Some have contributed in specific ways. Special thanks:

To my husband, Bernie, whose love and encouragement supported me throughout this project. I am grateful to him for the hours spent reading and rereading this text, correcting errors, and making suggestions.

To my friend Henrietta Lyons, who by her example is giving me lessons in aging with grace and humor, and who has always believed in me.

To Carolyn Jurkowitz, for not only being my cheerleader from the inception of this project, but reading and rereading the manuscript, giving me invaluable suggestions on style and content.

To Beth Srode, Mary Murray, Joan Floyd, and Cecile Landon, who read parts of this manuscript and gave me constructive suggestions.

To the staff of Antioch Writers' Workshop, Yellow Springs, Ohio, for their encouragement and valuable information about the craft of writing, and to my writing group at the 2001 Antioch Writers' Workshop for their helpful suggestions.

To June Cotner, for her expert guidance in developing the book proposal and her continued interest in this book.

To my editor, Maura Shaw Tantillo, for her interest in this project and her guidance through the labyrinth of pre-publication details.

To all the fine people at SkyLight Paths Publishing who have made my first publishing experience an interesting and enjoyable one.

Most of all, I am grateful to the One who makes all things possible, and to my spirit guides and angels, who have always been around me, whispering inspiration and reminding me that no book is written alone.

INTRODUCTION

As the New Year dawns crisp and clear, a bell goes off inside my head. Rather, it is more like an alarm. I am sixty years old this year! After twenty-eight years teaching and ten years as a hospital chaplain, my life no longer holds the unlimited possibilities that were at my disposal when I was young. Passing another decade, I see my life very much like a car that has a quarter tank of gas left.

Three options loom ahead. I could just keep going until I run completely out of gas. I could park the car along the side of the road, hoping that I will never use up the fuel, or I could acknowledge that the tank has a limited supply of gas and make plans about where I need to go. My choice is the latter, and now I have to decide where and how far I go with my quarter tank of gas.

People retire for many different reasons. Age, health, or perhaps a good retirement offer lead them to take this step. Whatever the motivation, retirement is a life-altering event for each person who goes through it. It is a new stage in life that touches every phase of a person's existence. It has physical, emotional, and spiritual consequences.

Although many of us long for this stage, and some envision it as idyllic, it has its pitfalls as well as its joys. How do we navigate this new terrain successfully on all levels?

As we plan for retirement some of us attend to every detail, while others are more casual as they dream about what they'll do when they retire. Financial planning may have been going on long before we actually retire. More immediate concerns may include moving into a smaller, more manageable home; establishing ties with medical professionals to help with present and future health issues; and joining groups of other retirees with similar recreational interests.

As a new retiree I have received in the mail many offers of books and magazines to help me prepare for this unique time in life. Conspicuously absent among all this material is anything about spiritual preparation. We are physical, social, and intellectual beings who have needs at every stage of our lives. We are also spiritual beings. We have spiritual needs, which if not fulfilled will leave even the best prepared of us feeling that something is missing. Our days may be filled with activities, but lonely moments will creep in, and we will question, "Is this all there is?"

Sometimes the word "spirituality" seems rather vague. Think for a minute about the fact that we are surrounded by a material world. The chairs we sit on, the food we eat, the air we breathe are all part of this physical world that encircles us. Just as we are surrounded by a physical world, we are also surrounded by a spiritual world. We just can't see it.

When I talk about spirituality, I am referring to the way in which we *recognize and relate to the unseen but no less real presence of spirit in our lives—both our own spirit and the ultimate spirit that many call God.*

When we move into retirement, we find ourselves in various stages of spirituality. As a chaplain in the hospital, I talked to many retirees. Some had a religious affiliation with a specific church. Others, no less spiritual, had a personal relationship with the Holy in their lives but not a specific church affiliation.

The real thrust of this book is to offer all retirees the opportunity to reflect on their spiritual journey, no matter what road they take. I hope that it will broaden your perspective. It is not meant to replace any present ways of relating to God that work well for you. Some people have a close relationship with Jesus. This is the way God touches them. Others have a relationship to a higher power as presented in the twelve-step programs. This book is meant to augment and enrich your spiritual traditions. Take what is helpful and leave the rest. Let your own inner wisdom be your guide.

Much of what I include in this book comes out of my own journey. I grew up in a small housing project in Dayton, Ohio. I was the oldest of three girls. My father, a freelance writer, was moderately successful; yet, raising a family when there was no steady income resulted in a stressful situation for all of us. Unfortunately, my parents dealt with that stress by drinking. As the years went on my parents became more and more preoccupied with their addiction and less and less able to respond to the needs of their three daughters.

We each dealt with this loss in different ways. As a first grader I was enrolled in the local Catholic school. In elementary school, large classes and the lack of any personal attention left me in a fantasy world of my own. As I got older I found myself more and more drawn to the church and school that provided me with some sense of structure and predictability in a world that felt insecure and chaotic.

It was not surprising that on completing high school, I made the decision to enter the convent. At seventeen years of age I joined the group of nuns who had educated me for twelve years. I made every effort to live well the life I had chosen, even though it was not easy. I did not expect it to be. I was very homesick the first year. I worried constantly about my family, knowing all the unexpected crises that can arise in an alcoholic home. This life was a big adjustment for me because as a child I had little structure in my life. Now, every moment of each day was planned. For a free spirit like myself, it took constant inner discipline to keep on track.

For nineteen years I lived as a Sister of Notre Dame of Namur. The convent afforded me a safe environment, where I had a sense of purpose and a feeling of belonging. A master's degree in education provided me with a solid foundation in my career as a classroom teacher and supervisor of student teachers. I found deep satisfaction and companionship in the field of elementary education.

Yet, underneath all the outward success was a river of unrest flowing from my childhood experiences and deep-seated needs. I became increasingly aware that I had entered the convent for protection, and I knew that it was necessary for me to leave the protective folds of the convent to prove to myself that I could make it on my own.

Along with this realization, a friendship had been growing with a priest I had worked with for nine years in the parish where I was teaching. Bernie and I had become friends as we worked together with the children in the parish. Over the years, that friendship developed into love, until we came to the time where we needed to make a decision about our future. At this point I left the convent and went to another city to teach. Two years later Bernie left the priesthood, and we were married.

I continued to teach until twenty-eight years in the classroom left me "burned out" and looking for another career. With my religious background and interest in people, I began preparations for a new career as a hospital chaplain. For seven years I served Mt. Carmel Medical Center in Columbus, Ohio. My work as chaplain was tremendously challenging and deeply satisfying. I often dealt with birth and death in a single day. Many of the spiritual insights that I will share with you in this book have grown out of my rich and life-giving experience as chaplain. It was a difficult decision to retire from this career, but I knew that retirement would provide me with the needed time to reflect, to write, and to accomplish some of my most cherished dreams.

Each chapter of *Creating a Spiritual Retirement* focuses on a particular idea for consideration from a spiritual point of view. It concludes with a poetic reflection and questions that are designed to help you see the idea of the chapter in light of your own life.

Although it is helpful to simply reflect upon the questions, you may gain clearer understanding by journaling. Journaling is simply writing a few lines or more about your thoughts on the topic presented. It is helpful to have a specific notebook for journaling. Dating an entry gives you the opportunity to go back and see how a particular train of thought has developed. I have adopted the practice of writing my journal as if it were a letter to my own inner wisdom, whom I have named the "wise woman." As I write to her I find myself speaking more from the heart. Writing has a way of coaxing out my inner thoughts and feelings in a way that simple mental reflection on a topic cannot do.

Perhaps you will want to use this book as a resource for a discussion group. Sharing reflections with others is a good way to open new avenues of thought. However you use it, I hope that you will find this book helpful on your retirement journey.

PART ONE

The Individual Spirit

1

Taking the First Step

So we make the decision to retire. Or perhaps we do not make the decision, but it is made for us by circumstances. Either way, we face a myriad of emotions about this step in life.

Perhaps we have a sense of euphoria as we think about lounging in bed far beyond the time we usually were walking out the door to work. We dream about all those days of choosing exactly what we want to do and engaging in that favorite pastime of golf or gardening. Unfinished projects smile happily, beckoning us to be their companion for the day. We are kids again, and it is the last day of school as we anticipate the long summer vacation.

Around the edges of the excitement and anticipation linger other emotions, which may rob us of some of the joy of the moment. Anxiety lurks around the corner. It may focus on financial concerns. "How will I manage on a fixed income?" Some of us who have few interests outside work might wonder, "What will I do all day?" Those of us who have developed our friendships in our work environment are haunted by a sense of distance and loneliness that retirement may bring to our life. Our relationship with these friends will

3

not be the same. If we deeply love our work, we may have an impending sense of grief at the thought of leaving what means so much to us. For most of us, retirement is a mixed bag and we recognize "all of the above and then some" in our decision to retire.

Recently I spoke with a friend who stated, "I will never retire! You know what happens. People retire and then they die!" I felt sad when I heard this statement. To this friend and to all who have made similar statements, I want to say, "Retirement is not the end of the road."

Retirement can be a time of new beginnings. We know of persons who have painted valuable art works, written prize-winning novels, and made scientific discoveries after they retired from their main career. When Anna Mary Robertson began painting in her sixties, she never dreamed that the work of "Grandma" Moses would become so well known. We may not all have such notable achievements. Freed from the responsibilities of daily work, we have the opportunity to develop new interests and skills. I know a man who had always been afraid of water. When he retired he not only learned to swim but now participates in the Senior Olympics.

Retirement is more than just a single point in time when we decide to leave the career that has occupied most of our time. It is a stage in our life journey, just as childhood or adolescence is a stage. It could typically span the ages of sixty to eighty, but no stage in life is truly bound by numbers. Retirement is followed by another stage in life that I would name advanced or old age. As with any stage in life, much of what we do in the retirement stage of life will affect the next stage.

Retirement can be a time rich in understanding of ourselves and others. It is a time to gather the wisdom we have gained through the years and make it our own. It is a time to take care of unfinished business. It is a time to look beyond the surface of our lives to the deeper inner meaning that is a part of each of us. It is truly a time to connect with our own inner spirit or soul and with the Great Spirit that animates all life. It is the time to gather around us what we will need physically and spiritually to sustain us during the last stage of our journey.

Reflection

This restless spirit of mine
has roamed my days and nights
in bondage
weeping.
She has served these sixty years
not in total slavery
for many times
she has spoken her truth
and her song could be heard
in the early morning.
She will have her freedom now . . .
well earned.
A faithful one she has been
to all my "shoulds" and "oughts."
This aging body trembles
to think of where she will lead me
but oh, what joy,
to die
dancing the rest of my days
to her music.

Take a few minutes, and sit quietly with no outside noise from TV, radio, or other distractions. Think about what emotions surround your decision to retire. Take each one out, and sit with it for awhile. You do not need to answer the anxiety or concerns that are raised; simply identify the way you are feeling. Perhaps you could then write in your journal or talk with a friend or family member about your feelings. It is important to look your emotions in the eye and sit with them. Like it or not, they are your constant companions.

If you had no restrictions and could do anything you wanted with your retirement time, what would it be? If you cannot do all of what you want, what part of this dream can you make come true?

2

Letting Go of Who We Were

IN RETIREMENT WE EMBRACE A NEW WORLD, BUT THAT MEANS letting go of a part of who we were. When we retire we all have to let go of something. Whether we were truck driver or teacher, manager or mechanic, clerk or coach, we were someone. We had a role, and we, as well as others, often thought of ourselves that way. Many of us identified very strongly with this role.

Suddenly that role is taken away, and a part of ourselves goes with it. While there are many beneficial aspects of our new state in life, retirement is also a loss. Just as with any loss, we must go through a grieving process. The depth and intensity of this process will depend on the circumstances of each individual.

One day we may find ourselves in denial as we hop out of bed and are half dressed before we realize we are not going to work today—or any day in the future. A gnawing sense of sadness sets in after a loss. If we have had a good working relationship with our co-workers, we may miss them and feel lonely. If we were prematurely terminated and forced to retire, we may be dealing with a lot of anger.

9

Another day we may feel disoriented and restless. Even though we have our list of projects, nothing appeals to us. We just can't seem to get anything done. One of my goals in retirement was to write this book. I was full of ideas and just itching to get started as soon as my responsibilities at the hospital had ended. Yet, during the months following my retirement, I was surprised that I had a hard time sitting down and actually writing. I felt as if the child inside me had just been let out for summer vacation. Often I simply wanted to do less demanding things, such as reading a novel or working a jigsaw puzzle.

Eventually I began to feel guilty about not writing—as if somehow I had betrayed myself. I decided that I would sit in front of the computer for an hour every day and write, no matter what. Of course, then I watched the clock, and it became the longest hour of the day. My husband kept assuring me that the writing would come when the time was right. He understood better than I did that I simply was not ready to start the book. My body, mind, and spirit were engaged in grieving the loss of my professional self. After about ten months, the ideas began flowing, and so did the writing.

All the feelings mentioned in this chapter are earmarks of grieving. Only time and patience will help us heal. We should choose activities that are not demanding, leaving ourselves time to be with our feelings. Such activities may include gardening, cleaning out closets, painting, or some hobby that leaves our mind free.

The grieving process is not something we can escape but an experience that must be lived through. We will have good days and bad days, but if we are willing to be with our feelings and be patient with ourselves, this too shall pass!

If we have been involved in service work all our lives, we are especially prone to feelings of uselessness when we retire from such a career. The very meaning of our lives was defined in serving others, and we may feel as if our life no longer holds meaning. If you are one of these people and are tempted to run out and volunteer—stop! Give yourself time—at least enough time to finish this book.

In some cases, we may give ourselves time and space, but our children or grandchildren may look at us and say, "Isn't this great! Mom and Dad are retired, so they can take Johnny after school every day until I get home from work." Or maybe we feel that we should take Johnny every day now that we are not working.

It is time to address our own needs for time and space. If not now, then when? We need to look deeply into our own hearts and honestly answer the question: "Do I want the responsibility of a child every day after school? How often? Once a week? Not at all?"

Change—even good change—is stressful. Our bodies also react to change. It is important to remember our physical needs, too. Exercise, eating properly, getting the sleep we need are all part of healing our grief.

Maybe it is time to cultivate our own garden before we go out and help someone else. If we are willing to do so, there is a rich harvest ahead.

Reflection

I opened the closet door
and there they were . . .
suits and dresses
standing like silent sentinels
in memory of a life I once knew.
Dressed professionally each day,
I went out to meet the world.
More casual and more comfortable now,
my garments speak of an easy day
with few deadlines to meet
and time between the daily chores
that make up my life now.
Yet I stand before that closet door
and mourn the death
of the one
who wore those clothes.

Picture yourself back at your work. How strongly do you identify with your role? What do you miss about your work? What do you not miss? Do you recognize feelings such as denial, anger, depression, and restlessness associated with the grief process? How are they influencing your life now? You may want to note these feelings in your journal. Talk with other retirees about their experiences.

3

Finding Out Who We Really Are

EVERY MORNING OF OUR WORKING LIFE, WE STOOD BEFORE THE mirror to shave or put on makeup. Rarely did we really see the person in that mirror, and more rarely still did we reflect on the existence of the person who looked back at us. We focused on finishing the task and moving on to the next activity in our busy day.

Retirement has a way of slowing life down. Lately, as I engage in those early-morning mirror sessions, I find a person staring back at me. Who is she, anyway? As I look more deeply into that mirror it seems as if a stranger is looking back at me. I hasten to identify that person. Bernie's wife? Melinda's sister? Jim's friend? Certainly all of these are true. Each person to whom I am related in some way tells me who I am. But this is only part of the picture. I am a writer, and even though retired, I am in some sense still a teacher and chaplain. Every job I have ever had defines, in some sense, who I am. But that is not all.

As I explore my identity I find many new avenues to walk. I can define myself by my hobbies and leisure interests, my geographic location, my gender or ethnic background. The more I explore this line of thought, the more multifaceted the picture becomes.

Imagine that we are in school standing before a large chalkboard. On it we are busily writing every word we can think of that defines who we are. When we are satisfied that we have completed the task, the teacher asks us to erase the titles one by one. After each title is erased, the teacher asks, "Are you still you?" What happens after the last title is erased? Are you still you? Who stands before the chalkboard now?

We are composed of many layers. As we peel away layer after layer of roles we come closer to the center of who we really are.

When I look carefully into the mirror, I sense that I am more than what I see. *There is an unseen part of me that is very real yet not visible to my human eyes. I define this unseen reality as soul or spirit.* This reality goes beyond the physical and even beyond thoughts and emotions.

I am aware that the recognition of a spiritual element in my being is not unique to me. From the origins of humankind to the present day, we have seen people expressing beliefs about the idea of an unseen reality, which they have often referred to as spirit or soul. This recognition of spirit was and is often expressed in rituals surrounding birth and death.

While we are physical beings with thoughts and emotions, we are also spiritual beings. Body and spirit go hand in hand to make us who we are. It is easy to be aware of our bodies. It is more difficult to perceive the spirit part of us.

One way we most vividly become aware of spirit is in its absence. Death is the separation of body and spirit. As we observe the phenomenon of death, whether of a loved one or of a stranger, we are aware that something that was there is gone. As we observe the body motionless and still, the source of life is gone.

That part of the person from which energy flowed and fueled the actions of the body is gone. From this perspective, I am left with many questions about the nature of my spirit. Is my spirit more permanent than my body? What happens to my spirit after it leaves the body? Why am I not more aware of the presence of my spirit? As I ponder these questions, I walk a little more carefully and with wonder at the mystery within me.

Reflection

A new day dawns
and I am left standing
outside the circle
of all the world says is meaningful.
I watch at a distance
as people hurry to work
and enter into the noise of life.
I am standing here
looking out on where I was yesterday.
Around me is time and space.
Will it be a vast and lonely place
or will I create
a sacred place in which to dwell?

Pause for a few minutes, and think about the many different ways in which you look at yourself and are identified by others. Imagine that these are written on a chalkboard. Your list may include your name, age, sex, ethnic background, career, talents, and other identifying qualities. You may want to list in a special section of your journal who you are in relationship to others. Imagine now that all these titles are erased. Are you still there? Who is it who now sits in front of this chalkboard?

4

The Round House

I HAVE ALWAYS BEEN FASCINATED WITH ROUND BUILDINGS, especially houses. Let us use the symbol of a round house to represent our life before retirement. Around the outside of the house are rooms called "doing." These rooms represent all the activities of our employment and our lives. Many activities can be placed here, depending on the type of work we did. If you were a salesperson, your rooms would have such activities as meeting, communicating, ordering materials, and traveling. If you were a homemaker, your activity rooms might contain such tasks as cleaning, cooking, washing, and ironing. These are the rooms where you spend most of your working day.

Inside the outer rooms is another circle of rooms entitled "thinking" and "feeling." Many times we are alone in these rooms of thinking and feeling, solving a problem or making plans for a project. It is in the "thinking and feeling" rooms that we experience the stress of deadline and responsibility. This is where we may encounter the frustration of being overworked and underpaid. If we are lucky, this is also where we find success and a feeling of pride in our work and in our lives.

There are many doorways between these rooms, and we move easily from one room to another. Sometimes we have one foot in each circle of rooms. As we wash the dishes we reflect on a pleasant trip we had. As we attend a meeting our feelings are smarting over a remark made by a friend.

We are all familiar with both the action rooms and the thinking and feeling rooms. The place that is less familiar is the solid circular room in the center of our being. This room is where our spirit dwells. Some people are not even aware that such a place exists. Others are aware of its existence but have stepped very carefully around it. Still others would like to enter but cannot find the door.

Access to this special place is available to all of us. Let us take a closer look at this central room that represents our spirit. Here is the powerhouse of our being. The room in which our spirit dwells is the center of light for the entire house. Streams of spirit emanate from this room to all our feeling, thinking, and acting. From here we receive strength and motivation to live our lives. It is the light from our spirit that adds clarity to our thoughts and feelings, helping us to better understand what is going on in our lives.

Whether we are aware of it or not, our spirit has enlightened and motivated our existence all our lives. At many times in our work and personal life, we faced stress and pressure. We look back and wonder how we survived those days. At other times, we saw a situation with lightning clarity. All along, our spirit was strengthening and guiding us.

The truth is that our spirit is always working in our lives, whispering to us in the depth of our hearts and urging us toward those actions that will bring about our good and the good of others.

Reflection

You, gentle spirit, are here.
As I walk through this forest of feeling
I carry your light
like a small star
cupped in my hands.
With this handful of spirit,
the night has light enough to see
and the next step is made visible.
This cup of spirit-light
dispels the creatures of the night
and warms my heart.

Find a quiet place where you will not be distracted. Close your eyes, and imagine the round house described above. Walk through the outer rooms, and observe yourself in the various activities of the day. What are you doing? Move into the next circle of rooms, and observe your thinking and feeling. These rooms are lit by a light coming from the central or innermost room. You see the door to the central room and open it. You walk into the light. Where is the light coming from? What does the room look like? What does it feel like to be there?

5

Gone Where?

IT SEEMS UNIVERSAL AMONG MY FRIENDS THAT ONE OF THEIR first retirement activities is to tackle those boxes and drawers full of old pictures. Those stacks of photos are a real trip down memory lane, yielding scrapbooks for grown children and some mystery photos to be identified.

As I sorted out my pictures the other day I found a faded photograph of a young man in the uniform of a World War I soldier—my Uncle Joe. It is hard to think of him as a young man because I did not know him until his marriage to my aunt, his third wife, at the age of seventy-two. He was a dynamic person and loved life. He walked two miles every day and hoped to live to see the age of one hundred. Although he fell short of his goal, dying at the age of ninety-seven, his life was an inspiration to all who knew him. He lives on in my memory and in the letters he left. I believe that his vibrant spirit continues to live also, on another plane of existence.

As we reach the age of retirement we all experience the loss of relatives and friends. Perhaps we have lost a spouse or the person closest to us. Sometimes, as we look at the photos and mementos we have saved, we have a sense that the loved one lives on. Something about them is indestructible. We know it is not the body. The essence of who they are lives on in their spirit.

Even though the spirit is not material, it is nonetheless real. We are so accustomed to thinking of ourselves as physical beings that it is difficult to understand that our spirit is more real than our body. Our physical body is simply clothing for the spirit. This clothing will one day wear out and be discarded, but who we really are continues to live on in our spirit. We, as spirit, continue to live after the death of the body. We continue to pursue learning and growing in another place. We call this place home.

Upon our arrival home, we will realize we have been here before. This home, which is far superior to the physical world, will be very familiar. We will recognize that this is the place we left before we came to earth. Here, we will have the opportunity to look at the life we have just completed, without judgment or criticism, and evaluate what we have learned and how we have met our goals for this lifetime. It is very likely that this is not the first trip we have made to earth, nor will it be the last.

If the idea of coming back to earth again and again (reincarnation) is difficult for you, you are not alone. I too have struggled with the concept that "I" could have been someone else in a previous lifetime. A trip through the family photo album helped me to understand this concept a bit better. It is hard to believe that the smiling baby girl my mother held was me. I have no memory of the day my mother sat me on her knee and my dad took the picture, but I have no doubt that it was me. The picture of the three-year-old eating Easter eggs with a friend is a bit more familiar, and the seven-year-old in the Communion dress is well remembered. The young woman, now clothed in the nun's habit, smiles proudly for the camera. As I look at the picture of the couple on their wedding day, my life as a nun seems very long ago.

Each of these pictures brings back memories of a different stage in this lifetime. Each stage has been integrated into the person I am today. I would not want to go back and relive any of those stages, but I am grateful for what each one meant in my life.

When we each go home, we will be able to look back and see different lifetimes, as I have done with the stages in this life. We will see how each lifetime contributed to, and became integrated into, the spiritual being we are now.

Reflection

When you left
all I knew was sadness
and a cemetery left soggy from the days of rain.
I wandered in a dark fog
looking for you.
Gradually the darkness lifted
and then I saw the curtain swaying in the breeze.
Only a thin curtain between us.
Your face plays in my dreams
and did I hear your voice just yesterday in the garden?
Your laughter weaves in and out of my memories
and into my reality.
The curtain sways and I strain
to see the figure
standing just out of reach.

Take out a picture of a loved one who has died. Recall some memories of this person. Have you ever had the sense that the loved one continues to live? Do you ever feel this person's spirit near you? Envision yourself as a small baby coming into this earth. Is it possible that a part of you existed before you came here?

6

Soul Purpose

OUR CULTURE TELLS US THAT WE ARE ALL HERE ON THIS EARTH for the same reason. The media continually bombard us with messages about being attractive, acquiring possessions, and having control. Many of us, at this point of retirement, look at these goals and measure ourselves by their standards.

Even though we have been successful in the eyes of the world, retirement and the aging process begin robbing us of some of our hard-earned progress. Power slips through our fingers as we hand over the reins of control to others. Our bodies age, and youthful attractiveness fades. A fixed income may result in diminished financial resources. As the power, money, and youth we have pursued slip away, many retirees are left with a fairly bleak picture. We feel we are at the end of the road looking back. It is like a roller-coaster ride winding down. The ride is over, and we are simply waiting for the end.

If we see our life in purely human terms, then we *are* at the end of the road. The truth is, there is a bigger picture. We, as spirits, made a conscious decision to come to this earth. We had a goal, which I will refer to here as soul purpose. There was something we wanted to learn or do that could best be accomplished only on this earth. While we may not be able to verbalize our soul purpose, it is written deep in our being. Instinctively we have always known why we are here.

Recall the central room of the round house. Within this inner room of our spirit is the sacred book of our life. In it is written our soul purpose. When we enter this inner room, we get glimpses of our spiritual goals or soul purpose, and we have an opportunity to evaluate our life in view of the purpose for which we came.

Recently we dined with a couple who have been retired for many years. The man spoke with sadness about how his health was limiting his ability to do the tasks he had always done with ease. He had been a very successful businessman and even after retirement had held various offices in different organizations. Now, he struggles just to take care of daily correspondence. His wife spoke about how he had often assisted various members of her family with their financial matters. With sad expressions they both agreed that those times were gone forever.

As they talked I looked at this man, and for a moment I glimpsed what I call the eternal present. I saw, sitting in front of me, the man who still "is" all the things we had been talking about. This is the successful man who helped others and held important offices. He is still the same person, even though he is no longer able to do certain things. Right now, he is doing other work that is just as important to his soul purpose in life, as he had done in his younger years. This gentleman has been battling ill health for several years. His fight to stay active has kept him going after many heartier people would have just given up. My guess is that those years of struggle have resulted in tremendous growth of spirit.

How encouraging to realize there is no end of the road in our progression toward our soul purpose, which is the reason for our being here. What we do today is just as valuable in our spirit's journey as what we did yesterday or twenty years ago. All along we have been working, consciously or unconsciously, on our soul purpose. In our retirement years we may be doing the most important work of our life in view of the big picture. Retirement is the time when we look deep within ourselves and refocus our energies on the goals that are most important to us.

Reflection

There is no reason any more
to rush from task to task
with eyes upon the clock
and hands unsatisfied because of work not quite complete.
For time
has suddenly stood still
and I,
circled round by space and time,
float gently in the present moment
sensing a deeper world
wrapped round my life.
And entering that world
drink deeply of contentment
and learn what my aging friends
have always known.
Only when time stands still
can we walk into life
and understand its meaning.

What do you think your purpose in life, up to this point, has been? Is there something else you need to accomplish before you leave this earth? Ask your inner wisdom to help you look at this picture. Use your journal to help you sort out the answers to these questions.

7

Taking the Plunge

AS I EXPLORE THE SUBJECT OF SPIRITUALITY I SEARCH FOR WAYS TO present it in a more concrete way. Unfortunately, we have no language to "speak spirit." What I have found are experiences here on earth that mirror and further broaden my understanding of the spiritual world.

One such experience happened when my husband and I were visiting Gulf Shores, Alabama. We stopped at the Down Under Shop, which taught diving and sold diving equipment. The staff graciously lent me a training video they used with their students.

As I watched the video I was struck by the similarities between a dive and a spirit's journey to earth. Imagine the diver standing at the edge of the boat, contemplating his dive. This was not a spur-of-the-moment decision. Much training and planning brought him to this point. The owner of the dive shop told me, "It's a whole other world down there." I found myself imagining that same statement being said to those spirits who decide to take the plunge into the physical world.

How much like the diver we are as we stand at the edge of the spiritual world, waiting to be born. For us, too, this was not a hasty decision. Planning for the spirit's trip to earth began long before the time we were born.

A diver who prepares to make a dive puts on special clothing and equipment that will help him or her survive under the water. We, too, clothe our spirits with this body in order to participate in human life on this earth. Without the special equipment of our bodies, we would be unable to participate and interact on this human plane.

While the equipment the diver uses is absolutely necessary to survival, it is awkward and limiting. The mask limits the diver's movements and ability to communicate. Communication is done by hand signals, and the finer nuances of communication must be left until the diver surfaces. We may not realize it, but our spirit, clothed in a body, is also limited in its ability to communicate. In this generation, we pride ourselves on our vast communication network, yet it is nothing compared to the lightning swiftness of spirit-to-spirit communication. Without the encumbrance of the body, spirits communicate by thought. There is no need for words, as the meaning intended is easily communicated between spirits.

The diver, descending into the murky depths, does not see with the clarity experienced on the boat. He or she encounters new, strange, fascinating creatures. The diver deals with shadows and dangers not present in the sunlight. Life on this earth has its parallels. We easily become engaged with all we see and are so absorbed in the physical that we lose all sense of the spiritual. We often deal with darkness and lack of clarity in our lives. We truly cannot see why things are happening.

The diver depends on those in the boat above for many aspects of the dive. They supply and protect the oxygen line.

They send a signal down if a storm is approaching. If the diver should become incapacitated, they will perform a rescue operation.

When we took the plunge and came to this earth, we were not forgotten by the spirits we left. Some of them are watching over us in the "boat above." We are never truly alone.

When the dive is over and it is time to return to the boat, the diver gradually rises toward the light, breaks the surface, climbs aboard the boat, and removes the mask with a sigh of relief, happy to be in familiar surroundings again. The diver breaths deeply of the fresh sea air and then discusses the experience with his or her colleagues.

When our time on earth is over, we too will rise toward the light. We will return to a place that is familiar and comfortable. Others will meet us and help us evaluate our time on earth. Perhaps we will plan another "dive."

This metaphor, like other examples, has its limits, but I do think that many natural experiences can speak to us about the spiritual world. If we begin looking for examples in our lives, they will reveal themselves to us.

Reflection

All I know
has come through these five gates:
the touch of sheets,
and smell of new-mown grass,
the taste of honey on my tongue,
the sight of hyacinth in bloom,
and sound of crickets on a summer eve.
But sometimes
I hear distant music and memories of a yester-life
and wonder if there is another gate
crafted quite differently from the five I know.

Does any part of this metaphor speak to you about your own life? Can you think of other metaphors that might illustrate your own spiritual beliefs and understandings?

8

Connecting with Spirit

WHEN WE REFLECT ON THE CONNECTION BETWEEN BODY AND
spirit, we realize that the two are interdependent. The spirit is
the life-force of our body. Without the presence of spirit, our
body would not be breathing and our heart would stop
beating. On the other hand, our spirit could not operate or
interact in a material world without our body.

Think for a minute about your heart. You have lived quite
intimately with this organ all your life. You have never seen
your heart, but you have no doubt of its existence—not only
because medical science tells you, but because you have felt
and heard its beating. You probably don't spend much time
thinking about your heart; yet, every moment of your
existence depends on its beating.

Our spirit, like the physical organ of the heart, has been
with us all our lives, and we depend on it for our very
existence. Although we cannot see our spirit, we know, on the
authority of spiritual teachers, that it exists. We also know
because there are times when we have experienced our spirit
directing our life in subtle and not-so-subtle ways.

The action of your spirit is written in your history. Take your working life, for example. Where did you find the strength to get up each morning, day after day, year after year, and go to work? Even for those who enjoy their work, this is an amazing feat. There were times in your work life when you had to make tough decisions that took both courage and insight. Perhaps it was the decision to resign and look for a new job, or change direction in your career. It was the light of your spirit that led the way.

There are other moments when something unusual happens. Which of us has not acted quickly and appropriately in a crisis? Later, reflecting on our action, we wondered how we knew what to do. At the time we did not question the message that came to us swiftly and clearly.

It is not just in the crises and big decisions of our lives when we experience spirit. The subtle presence of our spirit is with us every day. Quietly, our spirit walks with us on our daily rounds, supporting and encouraging us to fulfill the purpose for which we came to this earth. We often feel that presence but may not always name it spirit.

I became aware of the abiding presence of spirit in one of the most difficult years of my life. In September 1973, I was a religious sister teaching first grade in a local Catholic school. The school year was going well when I became ill, and surgery was scheduled for January 1974. The recuperation resulted in my absence from the classroom for a long time. This was especially upsetting for me because I knew I would be leaving this school and the convent in May.

I did leave the convent at the end of May and began the difficult adjustment of living in an apartment after nineteen years as a nun. Three weeks after I left, my mother died of a heart attack. As my dad and I struggled with our grief I began a new job as an educational supervisor in a treatment center for emotionally disturbed children.

I was trying to cope with adjustment to a new lifestyle, a difficult job, and the increasing alcoholism of my dad. My life felt like a nightmare. I wanted to die. I was convinced that all these events were a punishment from God for leaving the convent. I felt as if my life were hanging on by a thread.

Little did I realize at the time that the thread was nylon, strong and flexible. At the other end was my spirit. Then, I survived one day at a time. Only after I had a few years' distance from the situation did I realize the tremendous strength of my spirit, which had sustained me through that time.

When I was a chaplain in the hospital, patients shared their life stories with me. Often I was astounded at what people had survived. As they told me their stories I could see their strength of spirit. When I pointed this out to the patients, they would often come to a new awareness of their own strength. This insight was a source of courage for them as they faced their present illness.

When we reach the age of retirement, each of us can look back on difficult times in our lives. In various ways, we too have the chance to get in touch with that special strength of spirit that brought us through those experiences. When we reflect on our life experience, we realize that the silent presence of our spirit has been with us all along.

Reflection

You and I
body and soul,
melody and harmony,
words and music
we dance together
under the stars of this universe.
Like lovers
in their most intimate moment
we move through this lifetime
as one.

Take some time to look back on your life. Can you identify times of crisis or extreme stress? What was it like for you at the time? Can you identify times in your life when you have experienced extraordinary strength, courage, or insight?

Now is the time to perceive our
spiritual dimension—the strong, silent
presence of our spirit.

Now is the time to reflect on our lives
and recognize the strength of spirit
that has been there.

9

Finding the Voice of Spirit

OUR SPIRIT SPEAKS QUIETLY IN THE DEEPEST PART OF OUR BEING. It is not like the voice at the end of the telephone but comes to us in a thought or feeling. We have many thoughts and feelings during the day. How do we know which really represent the voice of our spirit?

I am helped to hear my spirit by getting in touch with the many voices that flow through my head. When I begin to name these voices, I can hear the voice of my spirit more clearly.

Perhaps you too have heard those inner voices that can scold, argue, shame, demand, encourage, or lift you up. They are at times in conflict with one another. These voices can sometimes be distressing and haunting and at other times comforting. They help me realize I am a multifaceted being with many wants and needs clamoring for attention.

Probably the first voice I became aware of, and could name, was the voice of the child. There was a time, especially in my adult life, when I would have been ashamed to admit that within me was a needy little child. I would have been embarrassed, because another voice was saying to me, "Grow up; don't be childish; act your age."

Much has been written about our inner child today, and I think it is now easier to acknowledge that the child is there. When I was in my fifties, a therapist named Marge first coaxed that little child out and taught me that I no longer needed to be ashamed of her. She taught me how to listen to the child's needs, reassure her when I was afraid, and discipline with gentleness and love. Today, I no longer deny her existence. She lives in harmony within my personality.

The second voice I came to recognize was the voice of authority—the voice of my mother, father, teachers, and pastor. This voice contains many old tapes that are played over and over again. They fall into various categories, from practical to philosophical. While some of these messages are just as valid today as when they were first recorded in my mind, others have outlived their usefulness. Remembering my mother's words about not forgetting my umbrella and wearing a hat on a cold day has certainly saved me some discomfort as an adult. Her angry words "You should be ashamed of yourself" are better off forgotten.

I learned to see God as a stern judge through the eyes of my teachers and pastor. Many of us educated in the 1940s and 1950s had the same experience. Pastors and teachers often used fear to motivate children to good behavior. Continuing to listen to this voice of fear will severely limit my ability to have a loving relationship with God.

Another voice that often interrupts my thoughts is what I call the perfectionist. This voice is demanding and accepts only the best work. This is a good thing in itself, but sometimes this voice prevents me from attempting a project, knowing that I cannot do it perfectly.

Every voice has its lesson to teach, but each one likes to set up a dictatorship by pretending that it is the only voice. All these voices need to be coordinated under the voice of my spirit. Here, each message is weighed in the light of my highest good.

If we are to hear and recognize the voice of our spirit, it is important to first recognize the many human voices that visit our minds. As we begin to recognize them we will prepare ourselves to attune to the voice of spirit, which is discussed in the next chapter.

Reflection

There they are,
like rag dolls sitting on a shelf
but far from silent.
The soldier with angry thoughts and sharp words.
The parent's disciplined command rings out.
The child is almost lost
crying in the corner.
Their voices rise in such disharmony
that I shout, "Silence!"
And in the stillness one strong sweet voice breaks through
and I am finally free to hear
the wisdom of my heart.

Have you heard some of the same voices described in this chapter? Perhaps you have a voice that is unique to you. What does each one say to you? Take one message you have received from your inner voices, and examine how it influences your life today.

10

Attuning to the Voice of Spirit

ONCE WE HAVE SORTED OUT THE VARIOUS VOICES THAT SPEAK to us in our mind, we come closer to recognizing the voice of our spirit. Meditation is one of the best ways to begin increasing awareness of spirit. In this chapter I will outline a simple form of meditation. If you are interested in further information, many instructional books and tapes on meditation are available.

Find a comfortable place to sit. It is better if your feet are flat on the floor and your spine is straight. In order to meditate we need stillness. This is a rare commodity in this age when television, radio, and the telephone continually invade our lives. We, as retirees, have the opportunity to turn it all off. If there is any time in our lives when we have the opportunity to seek stillness, it is now. Stillness means a cessation of all noise. It means listening not for the sound but for the silence. It is in this silence that we stand in the presence of our spirit.

It is a trick of fate that when we finally turn off the television and radio and establish an external silence, our mind speaks louder than ever. Our thoughts invade this sacred space with a thousand concerns. Suddenly there are pressing matters to attend to: an appointment that needs to be made, breakfast dishes left on the table, a thank-you letter to write.

If that is not enough, deeper concerns surface. We wonder how things are going without us at the office. Will our daughter's marriage last? Will we outlive our income? Should we really continue to live in this big house, now that the children are gone?

At this point, we can take certain steps to help eliminate these distractions and facilitate our meditation.

First of all, if something comes to mind that you are afraid you will forget, have a piece of paper nearby, and write it down. Then you can let it go.

Second, use your breathing as a focus of attention. Be aware of your breathing in and out as if you were controlling it. As you exhale, relax your body.

Third, close your eyes and visualize something that has a spiritual connection for you. One of my favorite visualizations is to think of the night sky full of stars. You may see yourself in a Buddhist temple, a Christian church, or perhaps sitting in the inner room of your "round house." The beauty of nature holds an infinite number of visualizations. Whatever place you decide to visualize, keep the picture in your mind's eye and continue to focus on your breathing.

Fourth, use an affirmation or mantra: a word, phrase, or sentence said repeatedly. It is important to choose words that are meaningful to you. Some of my favorites are "Peace" and "The love of God is flowing here."

You may not need all of the above suggestions to help you establish a focus in meditation. Perhaps just bringing your attention to breathing in and out will be sufficient to help you arrive at a quiet mind.

From this point on, meditation is a matter of "being" instead of "doing." You are simply there in the presence of your spirit. It may seem as if nothing is happening, but you are doing a most important work—attuning to your spirit. In this stillness you are learning to recognize and listen to the voice of your spirit.

I spoke of meditation as one of the best ways to attune to your spirit, but it is not the only way. Many people experience an attuning to their spirit when they engage in physical activity that leaves the mind free. Walking, running, and swimming are a few of the many activities that can provide the mental space to simply be with our spirit.

I have experienced the presence of my spirit in the process of learning about spirituality. Sometimes it is a book, lecture, or video that has opened a window within me to the spirit. Many fine books, videos, and cassette tapes on spirituality are available at your local bookstore or library. Just as everything about you is unique, so too is your spirituality. You will find some authors more helpful than others. Seek out those materials that resonate with your spirit.

In this chapter I have mentioned some ways to attune to your spirit. If you have not thought much about your spirit until now, these activities can get you started. Be aware that as a unique individual, you are continually discovering new windows to the spirit. Ask your spirit to guide you in your search. You may be surprised at the results!

Reflection

During the day
you speak to me
like the melody
of a half-remembered song.
You whisper in my ear
and through the noise of my mind
my heart
strains to listen.

You have probably been attuning to the spirit all your life but did not think of it in exactly those terms. What is it in your life that helps you regain and maintain your peace of mind? Perhaps it is something you do, or a place where you go. Try to identify what helps you become more centered and in tune with your spirit. You may want to experiment with meditation by establishing outer and inner stillness and focusing on your breath or a mantra.

11

Fruits of the Spirit

WHEN WE HAVE SPENT TIME ATTUNING TO OUR SPIRIT, WE WILL begin to notice differences in our lives. They will be positive differences that will contribute to our quality of life. Gradually we will come upon new insights that will bring us greater peace and contentment.

Sometimes we spend years in a job that yields little satisfaction. Financial concerns, seniority, or the fear that we are unable to do anything else may hold us there. Now, as retired people, we can choose our daily activities from the inside out. We can consult our inner wisdom and search out what we really want to do.

As we attune to our spirit we begin to see meaning and purpose in what is happening to us now and what has happened to us in the past. Although I did not recognize it at the time, every major change in my life was accompanied by a strong inner knowing. My decision to make a change did not always make sense to others, or even to my more practical self. I could not verbalize the reasons for my decision, but I knew I was moving in the right direction. Now, as I look back on my life, I can see a pattern of being led into situations that gave me greater growth and satisfaction.

Our spirit is the source of our creativity. As we live more in harmony with our spirit we will be more creative in all areas of our life. The mother of my friend spent her life making a home for her husband and five children. When the children were out of the nest, she took up oil painting. She had never taken lessons, but she produced paintings that amazed everyone who knew her. Each of us has witnessed persons whose creativity has blossomed in their retirement years.

This creativity may not play out in a particular art form, but it may reveal itself in our cooking, woodworking, sewing, crafting, or even the way in which we organize our time and energy.

As we attune to the spirit within we will begin to see the Holy all around us. We may become aware of it in nature. At times the earth will seem to glow with an inner beauty. We will come to realize that the Great Spirit is the source of all spirit, and we will recognize the oneness of our spirit with the Great Spirit. We will perceive the spirit of others and have a deeper understanding of how we are all connected.

Our lives will continue to be subject to all that is human. We will know pain and loss. At times our hearts will be broken. Through all of this, we will recognize our powerful spirit walking with us. In the challenges of life, our spirit will give us wise counsel, and in crisis we will find strength. We will know a greater peace and contentment in the present moment.

All that I have just written is not foreign to us. We have been experiencing the fruits of our spirit all our life. Daily attuning to our spirit will deepen those fruits.

Reflection

The house is still
and in the early morning silence
time stops.
Dramas played out yesterday
are like still pictures
hung upon the wall.
And in the quiet
I can ponder
their meaning,
their lesson,
and their truth.

Think about the activities in your life that have been the most satisfying, whether in your work life or in your leisure time. Is there a connection between those activities and your inner spirit? Look back on the major changes in your life. What led you to make those changes? Do you see a connection between them and your spiritual growth? As you review the crises in your life, what motivated you to keep going? Can you identify spirit in all of those situations?

PART TWO

The Great Spirit

12

Preface to God

IT HAS BEEN A LONG JOURNEY THROUGH THESE BEGINNING chapters about spirit, and I can hear the question, "Where is God in all of this?" The truth is that God, the Great Spirit, has been present in everything I have described. Our magnificent spirit is the gift of God, the life of God in us. Within our spirit is the silent presence of the Holy One, whom I will attempt to make more visible in the following chapters.

In the very beginning of this discussion, it would be helpful to look at the words and concepts we use to represent God. Most of us have grown up with a word or words that represent for us the concept of Supreme Being. Perhaps that word is Yahweh, or Allah, or Great Spirit. For many of us, that word is God.

At some time in our childhood we began collecting ideas about God. Perhaps we were in a very religious family, where lots of information was collected. Perhaps we were in a family where the name of God was said only in moments of anger or frustration. The attitude of extended family and friends provided additional information about the nature of a Supreme Being. Perhaps society in general, and a faith tradition in particular, augmented our God concept.

We filed all these ideas in a "God box," which we kept tucked away in our mind with similar boxes of information about the world around us. Over the years we may have added to the information in that box, but many of us still continue to operate out of the concepts of God we brought from our childhood.

Who is God for us? Is God the stern judge or spiritual scorekeeper? Is God the master puppeteer who has written the script and pulls all the strings? Perhaps we view God as a less controlling being who has given us free will and honors that gift by allowing us to make our own choices. Do we experience God as divine parent, protector, or friend?

There is no better time than now, in our retirement, to take out the contents of our God box and become familiar with what we believe about the Holy in our lives. It is time to realize that what is in that box is our *concept of God* and cannot totally reflect a God who is mystery.

The mystery of God cannot be contained in a set of ideas or concepts. We can never know this mystery completely, but we can and do experience the presence of God in our lives each day. What we think and believe about God has a direct influence on our ability to experience this presence.

For many of us, the following scenario might describe our relationship with God. Imagine a child who, in the presence of the parents, covers his or her head with a blanket and cries at no longer being able to see the parents. Obviously, the parents are still there with the child. It is the child's blanket that must be removed.

Sometimes our beliefs are like blankets that keep us from recognizing and experiencing the presence of the Holy in our lives. Are we holding onto concepts about God that, when examined under the light of our inner wisdom, are no longer true?

In the next few chapters I will share with you what I found in my God box. Perhaps you will find similar experiences and beliefs in your own.

Reflection

An old box sits in the attic
covered by the dust of time.
Memories of another life
come flooding back
as I stop to examine its contents.
I am amazed that
after all these years, some things still fit.
Others should have been discarded long ago.
It is time to start cleaning house.

Take out the God box that you have constructed over the years. Examine its contents by writing down the ideas you believe about God. Are some concepts still true for you today? Are there some ideas you need to discard? At this time in your life, what do you really believe about God?

13

Strange Gods

WHEN I WAS A CHILD, ONE OF THE MOST VIVID PICTURES IN MY Bible study was one of people worshiping a golden calf. It seems that Moses, the leader of the people, had gone up the mountain and there had received the Ten Commandments from God. He returned to the people to find that they had constructed a golden calf in his absence and were worshiping it as their god. They were violating the very first commandment given to Moses: "I am the Lord thy God; Thou shalt not have strange gods before me."

Some of those commandments given to Moses, which dealt with honoring my father and mother and telling the truth, touched my youthful guilty conscience. But I knew I would never worship a golden calf. I took pride in being from an advanced civilization and in knowing the one true God.

At this time of life, I look at that experience and realize that despite my childhood beliefs, I have been involved with strange gods all my life. Perhaps it would be more accurate to say I have been involved with inadequate concepts of the one true God in whom I believed.

I don't remember any formal learning about God before the age of five. At that age, I was enrolled in the first grade at the local Roman Catholic school. There I first met God as the old man with the beard. I am sure there were some pictures in my Bible study book that reinforced this concept. I did not have any kindly old men in my life. The only grandfather I knew was rather stern, so it was difficult for me to relate to God as an old man. I learned that this old man was all-powerful and controlled all that happened in the world, including my life.

My concept of God was further expanded by a chart the teacher had in front of the classroom. On it was drawn a triangle with a large eye, similar to the one on the dollar bill. The teacher explained this as a symbol of God. The three corners represented the three persons in God, and the eye was a reminder of God's all-seeing presence.

Something about that eye stuck in the mind of this literal five-year-old. The Eye followed me and saw everything I did. I began to fear that all-seeing Eye, which seemed to have a lot in common with another old man who knew whether "you've been bad or good, so be good for goodness' sake."

As my religious education progressed I was taught that the laws of the church were also the laws of God. With so many laws to remember, I feared that I might transgress one of the laws and be the object of God's wrath. I heard about people who had had bad things happen to them as a punishment from God, and I did not want to be one of them.

From all I learned during those early years, God emerged in my mind as a kind of great policeman in the sky, who knew all that I did and expected me to be good. If I was good, God was pleased with me. If I was bad, I could expect to be punished.

Even then, the true presence of the Holy, which has always been with me, was trying to get my attention. I had an unusual experience when I was about eight or nine years old. I was walking in the woods by myself. Gradually all the trees and bushes began to take on a special glow. I felt an intense joy and knew instinctively that this was the presence of God. I don't know how long I was there. I wanted to hold onto that experience forever, but gradually the brightness faded, and I was just a little girl walking in the woods. I often returned to that spot, hoping I would have the same experience, but I never did. However, this experience planted a seed in my heart that blossomed only years later. I returned home and continued to relate to the God I had met in school.

Some people, during those first seventeen years of my life, tried to challenge my concept of God and introduce a kinder, more loving God into my picture. There were warm and loving people in my childhood. My parents did love me and showed their love in the best way they knew how. Since I was the first grandchild on both sides, I was doted on by grandmas, aunts, and uncles. I did know love, even at an early age, but a deep chasm remained in my mind between my experience of love from others and the God who reigned on high. I could not make the connection that the Supreme Being, who reigned on high, was the source of that love. Like a child who refuses to give up a worn-out doll, I felt much more comfortable with my initial version of God.

Looking back from where I am now in my spiritual journey, I see little that remains of those early concepts of God. Even so, I held on tightly to them throughout much of my adulthood. They did not die easily.

Reviewing the early years of our lives can help us better understand our present image of God. Is it possible that some belief about God we have always held no longer seems valid, yet we continue to hold onto it because it is rooted deep within our history? With the life wisdom we have acquired, now is a good time to examine our early memories of God and look for their source. Some may be as valid as the day we accepted them. Others may be outdated, and it is time for a change.

Reflection

You are the one
I tucked into my school-bag
each morning.
The one I memorized.
The all-powerful,
all-just
all-seeing One.
Greater than Mom or Dad
or even the President of the United States.
In my smallness
I hoped that I could hide from you
In the great sea of humanity.
I hoped your all-knowing Eye
would not see me
as when I tried to be invisible
in the crowded classroom.
But I was told that your Eye
sees all
and I cringed in my small sinfulness
knowing that you saw me.

Take a look at some of the beliefs about God that developed in your early years. How did you envision God when you were a child? Who or what influenced your concepts of God then?

14

The Journey Continues

NOW I CAN LOOK BACK AND KNOW THAT AT AGE SEVENTEEN I walked around totally unaware of the loving Presence that constantly surrounded and supported me. I continued to cling to my religious beliefs, which offered some certainty in the midst of an unstable family life.

Then, upon my religious horizon, came a wonderful idea! I would become a nun. This was the answer to a deep-seated need for approval by the Holy. Surely, the all-seeing Eye would be pleased. I was certain that there would be fringe benefits for my family. If I prayed every day, my parents would be cured of their alcoholism. This was the best thing I could do for them and my sisters. If I gave up everything, I knew God would hear my prayer. I also knew this was an acceptable way of leaving a home situation that was becoming more and more difficult for me.

It appeared a win/win situation on all fronts, so at the age of seventeen, I entered the convent and became Sister Michaella. I buried the old me in a new identity that I believed was more acceptable to the Eye. I took to my new life immediately. I embraced all the rules and regulations and tried my best to be a good nun. But somehow I began to feel heavier. It was as if my burden had doubled, and I was not any happier. Could my burden have been a reflection of the fact that now I had not only the Ten Commandments and the laws of the church to attend to, but also the many minute rules of the convent?

Gradually, I found myself even deeper in my struggle to please the Eye. I was no better than before, and I had a whole new set of rules that defined my everyday life. It seemed that being a nun did not make me more pleasing to the Eye but was more reason for God to be displeased with me. During my first three years in training, I had uncontrollable crying spells almost every day. My novice mistress said that the tears were simply a trial and I needed to just keep going. I was so afraid I would be sent home. That would be the ultimate failure.

At the end of my three years of training, I stepped into a classroom of fifty-two second-graders. At this point my life changed dramatically. I loved the children, and I enjoyed teaching. While my first year of teaching was challenging and exhausting, I was blessed with much support and friendship. My former eighth-grade teacher, with whom I had a good relationship, was now my principal. Experienced and caring colleagues helped the new kid on the block get through that first year.

As a member of a school staff I was relating more to others, including children, parents, and other teachers. I was happier than I had been in years. I was still not able to make the connection that it was God who had entered my life more fully in the presence of these new people in my life. I could not relate the creative satisfaction I experienced as a teacher with the One who is the source of all creativity.

My joy in this experience was tempered by the knowledge that I was not a better nun than I had been before. In fact, when I examined my conscience, I found violations in the rule of silence, and many evenings I was exhausted and slept through prayer. There continued to be a great gulf between my human experience and what I perceived to be the presence of God in my life. I did not recognize the Holy in all of this because I clung so tightly to my God box and was not willing to let go.

When we reached adulthood, many changes came about in our lives. Some of us continued to nurture a relationship with God, but many of us found that this relationship seemed to take a back seat to our numerous new responsibilities. We were not trained to see God in the day-to-day activities of our lives, and we relegated the presence of the Holy to an hour or two on Sunday.

Reflection

As subtle as spring,
love grows
in our lives
until one day
we stop,
look around,
and realize it isn't winter anymore.

As you moved into young adulthood, did you see and experience God differently from when you were a child? What sustained your relationship with God? How did the responsibilities of adulthood affect your relationship with the Divine?

15

A Bend in the Road

YEARS PASSED, AND I BECAME MORE PROFICIENT IN MY TEACHING. The work became less exhausting and continued to be deeply rewarding. During these years, religious life changed, too. With the advent of Vatican II, traditions that had stood for hundreds of years were suddenly gone, along with our religious garb. We found ourselves in street clothes, engaged in activities that only a few years earlier would have been forbidden. The protective veil of the cloister was gone forever.

I found myself with confused and conflicted feelings. Sometimes I wanted the old traditional ways back. On other days, I felt we weren't moving fast enough toward our goal of being nuns in the modern world. The former schedule, with built-in times for prayer, was quickly giving way to increased social action and evening PTA meetings. God seemed to fade into the background, but I figured somehow I would catch up with the Holy when all the dust settled.

The dust never seemed to settle for me. While teaching full time I was also studying for a master's degree. After this I began training student teachers in my classroom. I was simply too busy to worry much about what the Eye thought.

If I had any guilty feelings, they were buried under the tasks of each day.

At this time, thoughts of leaving the convent began to surface. Two factors played a part in this decision. The first was a relentless feeling that I was hiding in the convent and needed to prove that I could make it on my own. Somehow, a "Molly" that I had buried a long time ago kept asking the question, "Why are you in the convent?" I had no answer. The second factor was the close friendship I had developed with an assistant pastor with whom I worked. During those nine years, Bernie and I came to know and love each other. This relationship changed my life. The experience of loving and being loved in return is one of the greatest human experiences. It can be a doorway to understanding the profound love of God. God was reaching out to me again, but I was unable to open the door. I could not make the connection between the love of this kind and generous man and the love of the Holy. I had made final vows, and Bernie had been ordained a priest. How could we leave our religious promises and not forever shatter our relationship with God?

As we worked together Bernie had become an important part of each day, and I realized that I could not imagine my life without him. He felt the same way. We had both come to a crossroads in our lives.

I left the convent in June 1974, and he left the priesthood in 1976. We were married that same year after having received the proper dispensations of vows from the Roman Catholic Church.

We continued to attend church each Sunday, and for me it was a kind of "soul insurance." This was what I had done all my life, and it seemed the right thing to do. I can't say I had a real relationship with God, who was out there somewhere beyond the great divide. Every now and then I experienced pangs of guilt as I felt the Eye watching me, but I was too busy to let that experience last for long.

A few years after we were married, I began attending a support group, Adult Children of Alcoholics (ACOA). It uses the twelve-step program familiar to those who have been involved in Alcoholics Anonymous and Al-Anon. The first three steps of this program asked me to admit that I was powerless over certain forces in my life, acknowledge that there was a "Power greater than myself" that could help me, and surrender myself to that Higher Power.

At this time I opened my God box to find that it was empty. I experienced a terrible loneliness. Even a stern God was better than no God at all. As I sat at ACOA meetings and heard people talk about their relationship with their Higher Power, I felt envious.

Then one day it happened. It was like watching a beautiful fountain rise in the middle of a pond. First slowly, then gaining strength, the presence of the Holy stood there, waiting to be recognized. This Holy One did not look at all like any god I had ever experienced. The Higher Power that I had discovered had no visual shape at all; yet, my inner being experienced a presence that was close, loving, and supportive. Then I realized that the God I had lost was not God at all but only my idea of who God was.

At about this time, Bernie and I began attending seminars at the Association for Research and Enlightenment (ARE), a community of people from all walks of life and spiritual traditions who have found meaningful and life-transforming insights from the readings of Edgar Cayce. Here we found elements of spirituality common to all religions, and we realized that God could not be contained in just one religious tradition. Our understanding of the spiritual world expanded as we were introduced to truths about the individual spirit and reincarnation. My relationship with my Higher Power was reinforced by what I learned there. We were taught to meditate, increasing our awareness of the Holy in our lives.

As we walked this spiritual path, authors new to us emerged to reinforce our learning and stimulate us to go further down the road. We began reading books by Deepak Chopra, Carolyn Myss, Thich Nhat Hanh, and Rabbi David Cooper. Our understanding and experience of God, the universe, and our own spirit began to expand. This transformation did not happen overnight but came gradually over the next fifteen to twenty years.

This is the road that has brought us to where we are today. This book is the culmination of what I have learned so far. Bernie has published his own book on spirituality, *When in Doubt, Follow the Yellow Brick Road.* We realize that we have not "arrived" in our search for the Holy but will continue to be seekers on this earth until that moment when our spirit returns home.

Reflection

God's presence
presses in on us
from every side.
Coming as sudden as a summer storm,
as gentle as a spring breeze,
as quiet as the sunlight slipping through the forest trees
in early morning.
It reaches through us
like the glance of one we love.

Did you experience a "bend in the road" in your adult life? Did a career, marriage, or children change your life significantly? What impact did these factors have on your relationship with the Holy in your life?

16

Will the Real God Please Stand Up?

PERHAPS YOU HAVE FOUND PARTS OF YOUR OWN SEARCH FOR THE Holy while reading my journey toward God in the past few chapters. If God is not the Eye, or the judge, or the great policeman in the sky, or the old man with the beard, then who is God? What can really be said about God?

Underlining all, the Holy One is mystery. It is hard for us humans to live with mystery. We "dig in" to the mystery of the Divine, desiring to plumb its depths, but in doing so we only find that we are swimming in a deeper mystery. This can be a frightening experience. Attempting to deal with an encounter that goes beyond our understanding leaves us dizzy and without an anchor.

For some persons, the best response is denial. It is easier to walk away from mystery than to deal with the unexplainable. For those who are willing to free-fall into the mystery of the Divine, there are rich rewards.

When we enter into this mystery of God, we have to be willing to accept that there are realities beyond those perceived by our senses. If we believe in our spirit, we have already passed beyond the confines of what we, as material

73

humans, define as real. We have come to believe in a reality that is unseen but no less real.

As we plunge deeper into the Holy, there are truths about God that surface. Women and men of many different religious traditions have been willing to travel this road and have shared their understanding and experience of God with us.

As I sit here writing this, a small chipmunk perches on the woodpile outside my window. I am reminded of Francis of Assisi, who taught people to see the Holy in all living creatures. The Dalai Lama has revealed the compassion of God in his passion for peace. Mother Teresa spoke eloquently of God's identity in her service and love for the poor. Rabbi Kushner looks at the highest and best in humankind and finds a window to God's Presence. Other peoples' vision of God can help us understand who God is, but ultimately it is our responsibility to take the pilgrimage into the heart of God and find the sacred for ourselves.

How do we take this journey, and what do we need? First of all, we need the desire to experience God more deeply in our lives. Our desire is the light that will lead us to the right path. It is the fire that lights the flame, our strength when we are tired, the hunger that sends us in search for food.

Out of that desire comes a request to the Holy. Our request that we experience God more fully can take the form of a prayer. We may find it expressed for us in our worship service. We may voice it deep in the silence of our hearts. Perhaps that request is an unspoken, anguished turning toward the Divine One in a crisis.

The roads that lead to the heart of God are many. Our religious affiliations provide us with a wealth of rituals in our pursuit of knowing God. However, God's presence is all around us and is not limited to one religion or ritual. You may want to choose a well-worn path that others have traversed, or you may want to blaze your own trail. Meditation is one path that has been helpful to many as they seek an experience of God. I have already outlined a simple meditation method in chapter 10.

As we pursue our understanding and experience of the real God, we need to employ both patience and openness. We cannot presume how and when God will reveal the Holy to us.

Even though we may talk about this experience as a journey, it is important to realize that we are not "going" anywhere. We are simply increasing our awareness of God who is already here with us.

Reflection

Mystery touches every phase
of our existence.
Faith enters
and love sustains this life
which we will never completely grasp.
This mystery
knocks out all our security
and leaves us groping before infinite truth.
Nothing can be bound,
no truth contained,
no person judged
for all contain an element of mystery
which makes them reach beyond
the power to
bind
or contain
or judge.
What greater gift can we offer
than a heart open to the mystery of existence?

Is there any experience in your life at present that is opening up a deeper understanding of God? It could be a religious ritual, a discussion group, a book, or a tape. Can you define what insights this experience has given you?

Now is the time to identify
who God has been for us in the past.

Now is the time to find out
who God is for us now.

17

Creation Speaks

As we contemplate this mysterious Divinity we realize that despite all the mystery in God, there are things we do know about God. Since the beginning of time, as we know it, we have acknowledged God as the creator. God is the beginning of all things, including ourselves, and that has lasting consequences for our understanding of who God is.

This God, who is veiled in mystery, has left clues about the divine identity scattered all over creation. Who is this God who warms my heart with the maternal instincts of all creatures and at the same time terrifies me with the strength of the ocean's waves plunging against a cliff? Who is this God who has designed the intricacies of DNA and flings universes into space? Who is this God who created the changing seasons that speak to me so eloquently of my own life?

Who is the Holy One that has spun the sacred web of body and spirit that we call a human being? Who is this One that has breathed the spark of divinity into my spirit that will live forever and has endowed it with the greatest gift of all—free will? Clues to the nature of this holy creator abound in the universe. Like good detectives, we must take the time to go searching.

Before retirement, in our busy and preoccupied lives, there was little time to discover those clues. Maybe that is why we enjoyed so much the quiet walks in the evening or that trip to the lake, where we could absorb nature at our own pace. Now, as our pace slows, the presence of the Holy around us has an opportunity to shine through this material veil.

On a human level, we can only create what is within us. The music was in Mozart before he wrote the symphony. The painting was in the inner eye of Renoir before it went on canvas. Life must be lived before the writer can write the novel. Every artistic expression tells us about the life of the artist. It speaks of the depth and beauty that lies within.

On the divine level, all of creation speaks of its Creator. All that we see was first a thought in the mind of God and expresses some aspect of the Divine. Creation is another one of those roads we can take to the heart of God.

Scientists are beginning to realize that the deeper they analyze their subjects, the more they are confronted with mystery. The human body alone is enough to provide contemplation for a lifetime. For me personally, the way in which all of nature functions can no longer be a chance meeting of atoms in chaos. They represent the work of the mind of God.

One reason I like to travel is to see the infinite variety and beauty of God's face. From the flowering desert to the immense stillness of the Grand Canyon, God speaks. I do not have to go to a faraway place to find the presence of the Holy. A sunny day in January or the first crocus of spring can speak just as eloquently of the Divine. The voice of the Holy, from the smallest bird to the wind in the trees, rings in my ears.

This journey to the heart of God is not always made on our knees with eyes closed and head bowed. Sometimes it is taken with eyes wide open to the greening of springtime. Occasionally this path leads through the latest scientific discovery. We may find ourselves on a wide, smooth highway or on the "road less traveled." Many avenues approach the mystery of the Holy.

Reflection

The cool of the evening
descends
washing down the heat of the day
and leaving pockets of mist
in the shallows of the hills.
Trees stretch up
like fine dark lace
against a dimming sky flung pink by the setting sun.
As I step to the rhythm of dusk,
God's presence unfolds
in slow motion.
The noise of the day diminishes
and night sound's gentle song begins.

What is it in nature that excites you? Is it a spring breeze or a winter storm? A rugged mountain or a calm lake? Does it speak to you about the Creator? Perhaps you would like to write a description of your favorite scene in nature, make a scrapbook of some of your favorite pictures, or, if you are talented in art or writing, put your feelings into a drawing or poem.

18

The Presence

I SIT BY MYSELF ON THE BACK PATIO AND WATCH THE SUNSET. There is a peaceful quality about this experience. My husband is out of town, and I am alone this evening; yet, I know that I am never really alone. In this quiet space I am aware of the Presence. "The Presence" is God with me. It is the holiness of God that surrounds me.

How does this Presence differ from the Eye? I perceive both to be always present, but there is an essential difference. The Eye was an invasive presence to be feared. It was watching me to see what I was doing wrong. This presence of God, unlike the Eye, is a presence without expectations. God is happy with me just the way I am. This is hard for me to believe, since I have grown up with the belief that I must earn God's love by changing in some way.

Who really wants me to change? Perhaps it is my family, my friends, church leaders, or society. It may be myself, but it is not God.

The Holy is here to walk with each of us, loving and supporting us in our journey. This does not mean that we are perfect and there is no room for change. It means that the desire to change must come from our own hearts when we are ready. The Presence is there whether we make changes or not.

If this Presence is always there, how do we become aware of it? For most of us, it is through our humanity—our body, mind, will, and emotions—that we know and experience the Holy.

A peak spiritual experience engages all the facets of our humanity. One such experience for me is the Holy Saturday Liturgy. On the evening before Easter Sunday, the congregation gathers in a darkened, silent church. Outside the front door of the church, the priest lights the "new fire." From that fire, a four-foot candle, representing Christ, is lit. The priest enters the dark church with the candle, stopping at various points for the congregation to light small candles they hold. By the time the priest reaches the front of the church, it is bright with hundreds of small candles. Participation in this ritual never ceases to be a peak experience for me. All of my senses are engaged. My mind relishes the rich symbolism of this act. My will again reaffirms my commitment to the Holy. My emotions are lifted, and my heart is filled with joy.

Like the changing seasons, our awareness of the Presence has its lights and shadows. Spiritually, we experience the high points of spring and summer, but we also have our autumns and winters, which are important to complete the cycle of growth. It is in this spiritual winter that we cry out, "Where is God?" and only silence and darkness answer us. At this time we may feel God's absence keenly, but we are no more separated from God than the baby who covers his or her head with a blanket and then cries because the parents are gone.

Sometimes our spiritual winter comes when some part of our humanity is struggling with difficulties. If our bodies are in pain, our emotions in turmoil, or our minds confused by what is happening in our lives, it may be difficult to *perceive* the presence of the Holy. At times like these, faith and hope, in the midst of darkness, are the only perception of God that we have.

As a chaplain I often heard people express this feeling. Weighed down by illness and often worried about family and finances, they felt distant from God. Some of them even surmised that their present circumstances were a punishment from God.

God's presence is not a feeling; it is a fact. We often associate feelings of peace, joy, and contentment with God's presence. The Holy is just as present when we experience pain, confusion, doubt, depression, and all those less desirable emotions.

Reflection

After the long trip
I sit quietly at the kitchen window.
Having journeyed many miles,
I really don't know where I am.
I pause
to read those inner road signs,
and find my inner sight
has grown dim.
Yet there is another vision
strong and clear.
You stand stronger now,
more real
than when I first met You.
I know your Presence
clearer than before.
You do not diminish those inner feelings,
the sadness, the confusion,
but you walk with me
and together we experience them.

Find some quiet time to reflect on the Presence with you.
Can you think of a peak spiritual experience in your life?
Can you remember a time when you sensed the Presence
in the midst of confusion, depression, or pain?

19

The Other

It seemed like just a routine day in the emergency room when the hospital chaplain was called to meet the family of a young man who had just been admitted. The patient, only twenty years old, had a self-inflicted gunshot wound and was just barely clinging to life.

The parents, brothers, sisters, and friends of the young man were gathered in the waiting room as the chaplain arrived. Their minister had also arrived and requested that the chaplain join them in prayer for the young man. Minutes seemed to stretch into hours as the anxious family waited. All eyes were on the door. A doctor and nurse approached the family. "We are sorry. We did everything we could, but he is gone." Quiet sobbing broke out as members of the group reached out to comfort one another.

Someone asked the minister to pray for the soul of the young man. The minister shook his head sadly and said, "It will do no good. His soul is lost. You know the teaching of our church. Anyone who takes his own life has gone to hell."

The room was silent. It was as if the family had been hit with a second mortal blow. Across the room, the aunt of the young man caught the eye of the hospital chaplain. She approached her quietly and said, "Chaplain, do you think my nephew is in hell?" The chaplain asked her, "Would you send him to hell?"

She replied, "Oh, no! I know him and I love him. He just broke up with his girlfriend, and I doubt if he was in his right mind when he shot himself." The chaplain responded, "I would not send him to hell either. Are we more compassionate than God?"

There are moments in our lives when we wake up and find God gazing at us from behind the eyes of another human being: the eyes of the nurse who gently tends us after surgery, or the look of a loving parent or grandparent. God dwells behind the eyes of those we love.

While we may come to know the Holy in creation and stillness, the human heart has the capacity to mirror God for us in a special way. We humans, made in the image and likeness of the Divine, have a tremendous opportunity to reflect the Holy to others. Many have responded to that challenge, and history is full of examples of women and men who have mirrored God for us. Our own decade has been blessed by the presence of such giants as Mother Teresa, the Dalai Lama, and Princess Diana.

One does not have to be famous to express the presence of the Holy to others. All of us could name a hundred acts of kindness by people in our own lives who daily express the goodness of God. It may be as simple as the person who stops in a line of traffic to let us into line, or as profound as the teacher who gave a kidney to one of her students about to go on dialysis.

We experience God in our lives in an infinite variety of ways, through other human beings. Falling in love is one way. When we fall in love, the human curtain is drawn back. How often have we seen a couple in love and have been tempted to ask, "What is the attraction?" We cannot imagine ourselves falling in love with that person, and yet the two people are quite contented with each other. It is definitely true that they see something in each other that we do not see. Perhaps for a time the human veil has been pushed aside, and each one is able to get a glimpse of the spirit of the other.

Sometimes it is difficult to get a perspective on this human manifestation of the Divine when the media continually report on the behavior of people whose human and divine energy has been misdirected. You only have to pick up the newspaper or turn on the TV to be aware of the murders, robberies, rapes, and discord between individuals and nations. Once in a while good deeds are reported, but in general the media is filled with sensational, negative news.

We have to realize that for every murder there are a hundred life-giving acts across the planet. A teenager makes a decision for adoption instead of abortion. A mother remains in a hospital bed, with feet up and head down, for six months so that her baby might have a chance at life. A husband patiently and lovingly cares for his wife with Alzheimer's disease. We don't have to go far to find the love of God expressed through the lives of human beings. We can look in our neighborhood, in our families, and among our friends. Through every loving, generous, and compassionate act, no matter how small, God reaches out from the heart of another person.

As we gather in groups, whether in our family, work, church, or community, we have the unique opportunity to take part in the mutual sharing of the Holy within us. The presence of God in us enables us to share the enlightenment, support, strength, healing, compassion, and love of the Divine with one another. In this sharing, we truly experience the meaning of holy communion.

Reflection

The sun hits the crystal
in my window.
Beams of color
shatter across the room.
As I sit in the glow
I know we are all crystals.
God shining through
sending holy colors
in all directions.

What acts of kindness have you experienced today? Don't overlook even the smallest. Look at those around you in family, work, and community. How does each of these people express the face of God? Can you identify ways in which you mirror God to others?

20

*

What about Religion?

THE ISSUE OF RELIGIOUS FREEDOM IS AN IMPORTANT ONE IN THE history of our country. Many of our ancestors gave up their homelands in order to find a place where they were free to worship God as they wished. Many of us have grown up in a religious denomination and have looked to our religion to be the gateway to God. We looked to its leaders to teach us about God and what God expects from us.

I spent much of my early life looking toward the Church to tell me how I was doing in my relationship with God. I thought that there was no way to God except through the Church. Sadly, I believed that there was no way to God except through the *Roman Catholic* Church. Needless to say, this resulted in endless debates with my young friends of other denominations. It is amazing that we continued to be friends under those circumstances!

A religious denomination is a gathering of people of like mind who wish to worship God in a specific way. One denomination is no better or worse than another. What makes a specific denomination good for a person is the degree to which it facilitates the person's growth toward God.

Maybe you have found a deep and fulfilling experience of God in your church. Perhaps it is through your church that you have come to not only know about God, but to experience God in the rituals and fellowship of your denomination. This is a blessing that is to be treasured.

No one can tell you which church is best for you. That is a decision you must make for yourself with the guidance of your own inner wisdom. Some people make the journey to God without the help of a religious denomination or church.

It is important to realize that a church is a human institution. It can speak about God but does not speak for God. At various times in my life I have heard stories of persons who will not pray or have anything to do with God because of what a particular priest or pastor has said to them. Their relationship with God was mediated through the minister. When the minister offended them, they took that person's words to be the words of God.

We are totally responsible for our relationship with the Holy in our lives that begins and ends deep within us. We dare not let a church, priest, rabbi, or minister take that relationship from us. The Presence is there to teach us and lead us. Some of us will be led to a particular religious denomination that will help us in our journey toward God. Some of us will choose to take a more solitary walk toward the Holy. Whatever choice we make, we need to test our path in the light of our inner wisdom and the Holy within.

Reflection

This road to the heart of God
is littered with
steeples and sermons,
with prayers and pillars
that have been abandoned
along the way.
But deep within,
each traveler
has light enough to see
the Holy One
who is both Companion
and Destination.

Do you belong to a specific religious denomination now? Why is belonging important to you? Have you left a specific church at some time in your life? Why did you leave? What part has your church played in your relationship with God?

PART THREE

Practical Spirituality

21

Where Do We Go from Here?

IN PART ONE, WE EXAMINED SOME SPIRITUAL TRUTHS DEALING with the individual spirit. There we began to see ourselves not defined and limited by all our human trappings: our gender, career, social status, nationality, and so forth. We began to see ourselves not as just human beings, inhabiting this earth for a specified number of years, but as spiritual beings having a human experience. We learned that our bodies are simply material clothing for our soul; like any material, they wear out and deteriorate with age. Our spirit, the essence of who we are, is eternal and continues to live after the death of the body.

We have a spiritual purpose for coming to this earth. All that we need to accomplish this purpose has been given to us. Our spirit has been our inner guide all along. We have the opportunity to make our journey easier by tuning in to the voice of that spirit and following its prompting more closely.

In Part Two we addressed truths about the Great Spirit whom we call God. Here we had the chance to take another look at our concept and experience of God. Many of us have carried an erroneous concept of the Supreme Being for years without examining it. As we came to explore our most cherished beliefs about God, in the light of our inner wisdom, some of those beliefs did not hold up.

When we experience God as an unconditional loving presence in our lives, the vision of God as a "punishing judge" or "the great policeman in the sky" fades away. When we come to see God as mystery, we let go of the need to understand everything about the Holy One. We are willing to embrace the paradox of possessing, yet always looking for, the Divine in our lives.

At this point in our reading, we need to ask the question: What difference, on a daily basis, does it make what we believe about God and our spirit? Part Three will examine the following questions about the impact of our spiritual beliefs on our day-to-day existence: Do the spiritual beliefs presented here have any bearing on the nuts and bolts of each day's existence? Will the minutes and hours of our day be different because of what we believe spiritually? Do our beliefs change the way we perceive others and relate to them?

In retirement, relationships take on new significance. We have more time to reflect on their meaning in our lives and more time to nurture them. The chapters on compassion and judgment focus a spiritual light on our relationship with others.

What do our spiritual beliefs have to do with our fears, life crises, and eventual passing from this earth? We know that challenges lie ahead as we deal with an aging body and mind. Fears and concerns for the future are more in our thoughts than previously. Can our spiritual beliefs address these concerns? The upcoming chapters on fears and death attempt to answer these questions.

In retirement, we lay aside the work that consumed most of our days. In my professional life as teacher and chaplain, I never questioned the meaningfulness of what I did. Since I have retired, I find myself searching for meaning in what I do. Is life meaningful only when I am giving service to others? Chapters dealing with unfinished business, getting the job done, and keeping in step help us view our daily activities in the light of our spiritual beliefs.

The remaining chapters will explore the questions raised here. It is up to each of us to seek the guidance of our inner wisdom to find the answers.

Reflection

I walk through this labyrinth of questions
a seeker from the beginning.
Age slows my steps
yet I must continue
for this may be
the most important part of the journey.

In your reading so far, you have had an opportunity to examine your spiritual beliefs about God and your own spirit. Before reading the next part, it might be helpful to ask yourself these questions: "What difference does it make, on a daily basis, what I believe?" "Do my spiritual beliefs about God and spirit influence my day-to-day actions?" Jot down some of your answers.

22

Compassion 101: Loving Yourself

SEVERAL YEARS AGO, I ATTENDED A RETREAT AT WHICH THE LEADER directed us in a unique exercise. He told us to touch our eyes and to thank that part of our body for all those years of faithful service. We thanked our eyes for the years of eyestrain in studying for exams and being subjected to chlorine in swimming pools. We thanked them for the beauty they had brought to us and how our sight had kept us safe on many occasions. We paused for a few minutes and then went on to the next part of our body. We quietly meditated on how our ears had faithfully served us. By the time we had reached our shoulders, tears were streaming down my face.

How hard I had been on my body all these years, with never an expression of appreciation! For the first time I experienced compassion for my body. In doing so, I experienced compassion for myself.

After that experience I began to feel differently about myself. All those years I had demanded so much of myself and was critical when I did not live up to my expectations. I never thought to thank myself for what I did accomplish. I had always evaluated the results but failed to look at the effort.

I had often thought that eventually I would love myself when I was holier, smarter, thinner, or more attractive. I would love myself when I was more successful, more organized, or more popular. What a surprise! Here I was—loving myself just as I was with all my limitations. I was feeling compassion for all the struggles and sorrow that had accompanied my journey, and I was grateful for what I had accomplished.

Many of us see and evaluate ourselves from the outside in. We compare ourselves with others in similar circumstances. If we see ourselves as less than our peers, we berate ourselves for our deficiencies. Compassion begins when we can forgive ourselves for not living up to our "shoulds" and "oughts." Compassion begins when we can forgive ourselves for the mistakes we have made. Many of us carry a smoldering self-anger under a seemingly calm exterior. Love grows when we can recognize this anger and invest this energy into moving forward. When we can do this, we are closer to understanding how we are loved by God.

Whenever I think of God's love, I am reminded of my dear Irish grandmother. I can still see her smiling face and feel the warmth of her unconditional love. She knew I had a lot of growing to do, but she was able to delight in, and accept, who I was at that moment.

I believe that this is the way God, as divine parent, looks at us. We are a precious and unique spark of the Divine, and the Holy One accepts and embraces us just as we are at this moment.

When I entered the convent at age seventeen, I came under the direction of a loving and compassionate woman, Sister Cecilia. Over the years I have come to appreciate her deep spirituality. Much of what she taught me is still with me today. One of her sayings, which I did not understand then, has haunted me all my life. She said, "When you come to realize that God loves you, your whole life will change." I sought that understanding and was sure it would come before I was eighteen. But it did not come then, or when I was twenty-eight or thirty-eight. All my life I pursued that realization, but it eluded me. Only recently have I been able to truly say I have come to possess it. When I came to accept myself as I am, and understood that God loves me just as I am, I opened the door to the Presence that has always stood on my porch waiting to come in.

In that understanding, my life has changed. It has not changed exteriorly but interiorly, where we really live our lives anyway. Loved by the Holy One, I am valuable not for what I do but for who I am. Because I am a spiritual being having a human experience, my existence here is meaningful, even if I lose a leg, an arm, or my mind. My constant companion, whether I perceive it or not, is a compassionate God who will always be with me.

Reflection

This morning of my life
I wake up and put on this body.
More than clothing,
it is the vehicle that will move me
through this life's day.
It both hides and reveals
who I am.
It is all I have
to express the reason I am here.
Will I not be sad at day's end
when stained and worn
with the day's living
I must lay aside
this precious clothing?

Choose a particular part of your body, and focus on it for a few minutes. Perhaps you will choose your eyes, shoulders, or hands. Explore how this part of your body has served you, and thank it for what it has done. Over time, do this with each part of your body, and express your gratitude for its service. If you desire an understanding of God's love for you, ask for it, and know that you will receive what you ask.

Now is the time to reach inward
and touch our essence.

Now is the time to strip away
the many faces of the roles we have played,
and recognize who we really are.

23

Compassion 102: Loving Others

THE PREVIOUS CHAPTER, "COMPASSION 101: LOVING YOURSELF," is a prerequisite for this one. We cannot have a healthy relationship with others if we have not begun the journey toward loving ourselves. If we enter into a relationship with no understanding or regard for ourselves, it is bound to end in failure.

What is love, anyway? I seem to have spent many years looking for that answer. This shouldn't surprise me, since poets, writers, musicians, theologians, and philosophers have been trying to define love for centuries. Often they have said that love depends on the desirability of the one loved. The poet says, "I love you because you are sensitive and kind." The musician says, "I love you because you are beautiful." The philosopher says, "I love you because you are good." What if someone is not beautiful, or good, or sensitive, or kind? Can such a person still be loved?

I believe they can, but to understand this answer we have to change our thinking about loving. We have to reexamine the widely held belief that love depends on the desirability of the object. We need to see love as a quality in the individual who is doing the loving.

Love is a quality in the heart of the person who is loving. It does not depend on the attractiveness of the other. It does not depend on the actions of the other. Love depends on my ability to open my heart wide enough to embrace the other as he or she is. It is that part of myself that reaches out, in care and concern, for the welfare of another. It is that part of all of us that can continue to wish only the best for the other.

Something happens in the understanding of ourselves as we realize that love comes from inside of us. As we expand our hearts to include others we become more aware of ourselves as a loving person. As we envision ourselves as loving we become more loving. There is a positive snowball effect.

Now is a good time to stop and take a look at our relationships. No one arrives at the point of retirement without much life experience in relationships. Great joy and deep pain have all been a part of our experience with spouses, children, friends, and colleagues. It is possible that we are still struggling with painful and unresolved feelings. Our past experiences with others may leave us stinging with anger and resentment. Where does love come in when we have been hurt by another?

I believe that when we are armed with the love from within, it is possible to let go of the past, and to embrace those who have hurt us, by holding in our hearts a wish for their good. This is forgiveness. We can take practical steps to accomplish this. First of all, we can ask the Holy within for help. We can refuse to keep rehearsing the injuries others have done to us, and instead replace this rehearsal with a wish for their welfare.

When appropriate, we can initiate a reconciliation. It is important to realize that this is not always helpful. We have to look to our own inner wisdom to be our guide. Love does not ask that we become a doormat or allow someone to take advantage of us. Loving ourselves means that we have the right to draw the line and protect ourselves from harm. Ultimately, that is the best thing for the other, too.

In this chapter and the preceding chapter, I have equated love with compassion because I believe that compassion is the heart of love. Compassion is the act of reaching out beyond our own judgment far enough to let ourselves walk in another's shoes and experience her life from her point of view. From this place, judgment ceases, and we feel deeply with her struggles and triumphs. We do not try to change her or ask that she be different. We accept her as she is, and affirm the value of her being. We see beyond the human exterior to the powerful spiritual being that she is, and we respect her spiritual journey. We support her by walking with her. As we recognize the source of love within us and open our hearts to it, we will find that sometimes reaching out is easy and accompanied by intense, pleasurable emotion, and sometimes it is a pure act of our free will.

Love has many different degrees and ways of expressing itself. It reminds me of the basic dough that the baker puts together and then uses to make loaves of bread, dinner rolls, and sweet rolls. By adding seeds, herbs, spices, and sugars, the baker is able to produce a great variety of creations from the basic dough. The love we have for others will be expressed in an infinite variety of ways. All true love springs from the love of the Holy One that we have inherited from our divine parent.

The love of the Divine, which has been placed within us, is a light that is always turned on in our hearts. We have the power to direct that light wherever we choose.

Reflection

Drawn by common threads
we seek each other's presence.
We move across those threads
until our beings touch,
and in the intimacy of that moment
we discover our differences
a source of joy
and challenge in our relationship.

Look back on your life and explore the love in your relationships. What is it in the good relationships that have made them last? Are there relationships that are painful and unresolved? Is it possible for you to change your experience of these relationships by applying some of the suggestions in this chapter?

24

Judge Not Lest . . .

April 20, 1999, will live in the memories of most of us forever. The massacre at Columbine High School in Colorado was played over and over again on the TV. Shortly after the incident, the May 3 cover of *Time* magazine displayed the pictures of the two young men who were responsible for the shootings with this caption: "The Monsters Next Door."

I was shocked at the caption and immediately thought about the parents of those two students. What was it like for them to see their sons' faces accompanied by those words?

They were not monsters but teenaged boys. They were powerful spiritual beings just like each of us. What happened? The nation kept asking this question. Many people looked for someone to blame. Was it the fault of other students, or the educational system, or the parents, or the boys themselves?

There is only one true statement about all of this: *We do not know.* This is the one statement that will free us from judgment and allow us to offer support to all who were and are grieving in this situation, and in other similar ones. Even if we could put every human piece of this puzzle together, there is still a whole spiritual dimension of the situation that we will never know on this earth.

Thinking back over my own life, I realize how often I have judged others. When I think I know why people act as they do, I am judging them. When I label persons as good or bad, rich or poor, kind or mean, smart or dull, right or wrong, I am judging them. When I see people only in the way they relate to my life, I am judging them. I have come to realize that the windows through which I view others are muddied with prejudice and filled with labels.

One day, when I was driving with a friend, we observed a rather disheveled man sitting on the sidewalk, drinking from a wine bottle. I remarked that it was a shame this person had not made something of his life.

She replied, "Maybe he is making something of his life, and this is the way he is doing it." I looked surprised at her response and she went on to explain further. "Perhaps his 'soul' purpose for coming to earth is to learn humility. Before he came to this earth he made a decision to work at attaining humility through an addictive disease."

I began to ponder. Could someone who is so clearly a failure in the eyes of society really be successful from a spiritual point of view? If this were true, then I would have to start altering many of the ways I looked at others.

I stand before my window that looks out on others, and I am aware of how clouded my vision has become. I attempt to peel away the labels that have adhered to this window for so long, and it is not easy. It will take time and a conscious effort to recognize that each person is a powerful spiritual being, clothed in this physical form.

As I do this, something significant happens in me. I feel free, and I realize what a burden my need to judge has placed upon me. Now I simply look at the other as someone on a soul journey just like myself. We are fellow travelers in this world.

I do not feel impelled to change or fix anyone. I know that on some spiritual level we are all connected, and I wish each person well. As I attempt to clear away old prejudices and labels I relate in a more comfortable and open way to others. My life is enriched by those around me.

The phrase "judge not lest you be judged" has a new meaning for me. It seems that there is a direct relationship between my need to judge others and self-judgment. As I let go of prejudices and labels I have attached to others I find my attitude toward myself becoming more positive and less critical. I can recognize that inner judgmental voice for what it is, and value the information it gives me, without allowing it to rule my life.

We can all benefit by examining our way of looking at others. Forgoing judgment will open the door to compassion. This compassion will be directed toward others and ourselves. If we can replace our labels and prejudices with the understanding of all people as powerful spiritual beings, we will see good things happening within ourselves and in our relationship to others.

Reflection

When will I get beyond
seeing you
mirrored in my own needs?
When will you stand
an individual
in your own right
without the clothing of my expectations
and wishes wrapped around you?
Will there ever be a time
when my eye is so uncluttered
that I no longer trip over my own feet?

Examine the way you look at others. Do you find yourself labeling others? Do you judge their actions? The next time you are aware of these things, try to say, I do not know, and affirm in your mind that this person is a powerful spiritual being.

Now is the time to look deep within ourselves
and refocus our energies on the goals that are
most important to us.

Now is the time to love and appreciate
ourselves and others in a new light.

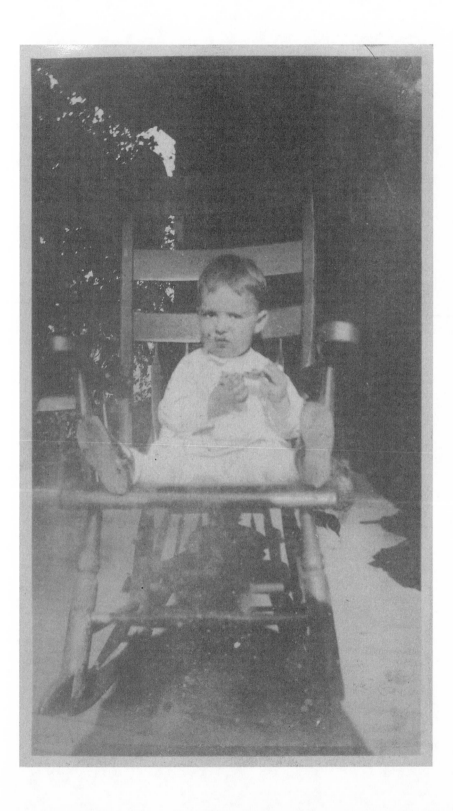

25

When Bad Things Happen

EACH DAY AS I TURN ON THE NEWS I AM REMINDED OF PEOPLE facing a multitude of losses. Recently a tornado hit about one hundred miles from our home. I watched people sorting through the wreckage and realized that I could have been one of those people. As devastating as the destruction of one's home is, it cannot be compared to the people of Kosovo streaming out of their homeland. How does one cope with the loss of everything—homeland, loved ones, identity, innocence? There is so much loss, it is staggering.

Some say that when bad things happen, they are a punishment from God. Others see misfortune as a trial sent by God to strengthen them. I do not believe that any of these unwanted circumstances are sent by a loving God. How, then, do we make sense of the losses we experience in our lives?

As a child I spent several summers at a girls' camp. Only seven years old at the start of the first summer, I begged my mother to sign me up for the entire summer. She did so with the warning that if I were signed up for the entire summer, she would not come and get me until the season was over. That first summer at camp had its ups and downs. I overcame a serious bout of homesickness and poison ivy. I loved swimming and horseback riding, but I hated clearing the tables after meals and washing down the bathhouse.

As the sweat trickled down my face on long summer hikes I wished I were at home. Many times I was tempted to ask the director to call my mom and have her take her daughter home. But I persevered that first summer, and at its end I returned home a healthier and happier child and begged to go again the next summer.

As I reflect on my summer camp experience I am reminded of another commitment we all made before we came to this earth. We signed up for life on this earth. In doing so, we became subject to all the ups and downs that are a part of earthly existence. We entered an imperfect world where, according to our human standards, things can "go wrong." We willingly set aside the memory of our spiritual home and friends to walk this earth in a kind of spiritual blindness. We contracted to travel this earth in a human body, subject to all its frailties and limitations. We came with the eagerness of a seven-year-old, to experience life on earth and to grow spiritually.

At the beginning of this commitment, I think we were better informed than I was at the beginning of my camping experience. Before we came to this earth, we knew that it operated within certain laws and we would have to live within the confines of these laws. Even with our spiritual nature, we could not suspend these laws but must be subject to them.

A simple example of these laws is gravity. Jumping from a height will result in injuries and even death. The human body operates by certain laws. Cutting off oxygen to the lungs for a specified time will result in death. We know that in an imperfect world, accidents happen that violate these laws, resulting in injury and death.

Probably the law that has the most impact on us is that of free will. All humans have the opportunity of choosing their actions. Unfortunately, others sometimes choose actions that harm us or our loved ones. Even though we are powerful spiritual beings, when clothed in our humanity we are subject to all the limitations of that clothing. There were no guarantees that we would be saved from suffering, sadness, loss, and physical death.

We may understand why we have come here and the consequences of our journey; yet, all this knowledge is little comfort as we face the inevitable and often tragic losses in our lives. When we are overwhelmed with loss, where can we turn? Death, illness, accidents, and tragedies lead us to drink deeply of the human condition. Often, at such times, all we can do is to search for something to hold on to as we feel swept into a dark and terrifying ride. That ride may go on for months or even years. It may last only a few days.

What do we hold on to as we struggle to stay upright through this confusing and dark time? For each person it will be different. A young mother facing the loss of her husband may hold on to the welfare of her children. These children may be the driving force that helps her survive the tragedy. A cancer patient facing the sure prospect of death holds on to his or her beliefs about life after death. Sometimes we don't know what we are holding on to, but there is something there— indefinable, yet real—that supports us. I believe that this "indefinable something" is the strength of our spirit, which is always with us. In the midst of the whirlwind or depressing stillness that follows a loss, the light of our inner spirit is always there to guide and comfort us. Simply put, we are never alone.

Each one of us can look back on those difficult times and, in retrospect, identify what it was that got us through. We can do more than that. As we review the losses in our lives, we can see the meaning and the lessons that experience had for us.

Retirement is a good time to look back on those dark times in our lives. Reflecting on our losses from a distance, we may discover new understandings and see patterns of learning that may give us clues to our soul purpose—our reason for coming to this earth.

Reflection

Without choice, like a bucket
I am lowered into the well of sadness.
Falling with uncontrolled speed,
I careen
into the black abyss
and plunge into the icy waters.
Numbed by the cold,
I am unaware of being filled
until I feel a gentle pull.
My spirit begins to rise.
Illusion gives way to reality.
The light and warmth of the sun touch me
as the bucket is passed around
for all to drink.

Take time to look back on the losses in your life. What was the most difficult loss for you? Can you identify what helped you through that time? Did you learn from your experiences? How do you answer the question "Why do bad things happen?"

26

Sitting with the Feelings

MOST OF US PROBABLY NEVER STOP TO THINK ABOUT THE tremendous influence our emotions have on our lives. Sometimes they are like the tail wagging the dog, and we don't realize it. Retirement is a good time to pause and take a look at our feelings. It is helpful to consider how they have influenced and continue to influence our lives each day.

In a single day we experience many different emotions. We are barely aware of some, while others demand our full attention. Emotions such as joy, excitement, satisfaction, and contentment may lift us up, motivating and energizing us. Just as strong in their impact, emotions like fear, anger, depression, and grief can leave us paralyzed and unable to act. Emotions fluctuate during the day. In the midst of pleasant feelings, less desirable emotions may enter like a sudden summer storm.

Our feelings of happiness may be rudely interrupted by a sense of frustration over a task that is not going well. After an argument, anger begins to smolder, clouding the warm feelings between lovers. Excitement over a coming trip turns to disappointment when the car won't start.

Sometimes we feel emotionally tossed about like a small ship at sea. We go up and down, looking for an anchor as we feel totally out of control. For many people, feelings seem to be their only anchor. Since they are changing constantly, life seems very unstable.

We do not have to live our lives being tossed from one emotion to another. There is a stable anchor at the center of our lives. Recall the symbol of the round house in chapter 4, and remember that our thoughts and feelings are not the center of our being. They are only a part of who we are, and they are built around a spiritual center that is firm and constant. Our spirit is the anchor we can hold on to when all around us is changing.

How do we gain access to this anchor in the midst of an emotion-tossed experience? One way to do this is what I call sitting with the feelings. The first step in this process is to sit quietly, focusing your attention on what you are feeling. Do you have a tendency to suppress, bury, or deny this feeling? Enter into the emotion, and experience it.

For example, let's say you are feeling anger. Sit in the presence of that anger. Be aware of how different parts of your body are reacting to the feeling. Is your adrenaline pumping, your gut churning, your skin tingling? This emotion has been asking for your attention, and now you are recognizing it.

At this point, it is important to feel the anger without feeding it. If you begin to think about why you are angry and how you will retaliate, then you are feeding the emotion instead of being with it. Thinking at this point will not help you, because in the grip of an intense emotion your thought process is clouded.

Once you have entered into the feeling and have acknowledged the presence of the emotion, turn toward your spiritual center. Perhaps you have created a visual image of your inner room. If you have, enter that room now, and sit quietly in the presence of your spirit with the feelings you have. Ask your spirit to help you deal with the feelings. Give yourself time to listen for an answer. Try to keep your mind clear, and simply focus on the presence within you. Often an insight does not come immediately, but eventually you will have a deeper understanding of your situation. Frequently the insight you receive helps you understand the meaning of the experience in the total plan of your soul's purpose.

When I was younger, I often felt ashamed of my feelings, especially my more negative feelings. I thought that if I were holier, wiser, healthier, or more intelligent, I would not have those feelings. I guess I thought perfection was walking around in some kind of emotional vacuum. "I should not feel this way" is a phrase too many of us have said too frequently.

At the time, I did not realize that emotions are powerful teachers and are a necessary part of growth. In retrospect, I can see this and even identify some of the lessons.

Resentment is an emotion many of us have felt at some time in our lives. As a young nun I sometimes felt resentful when others received special assignments to teach or study. One particular incident stands out in my mind. I was the first-grade teacher at a private school run by the nuns. They had just begun a Montessori program and were planning to send someone to study Montessori over the summer and join the present staff. They knew that I was interested, and I was sure that I would be the one chosen.

When the summer assignments came out, not only was I not assigned to study Montessori, but instead I was being transferred to Dayton, Ohio, to teach third grade the following year. Dayton, Ohio, was the end of the world as far as I was concerned. I was crushed with disappointment and resentful of the nun who was assigned to study Montessori. Little did I realize that my life was moving in the right direction. A young priest by the name of Bernard Srode was also being assigned to the same parish. I was not destined to be another Madame Montessori—but being Mrs. Srode was definitely in the cards!

My own inner spirit has led me to recognize valuable lessons from my bouts with resentment. I have come to realize that the Holy One will provide all I need to accomplish my purpose in life. I am always exactly where I need to be in relation to my soul purpose. Wanting what someone else has is a waste of my precious time and energy. Wanting to take away what someone else has deprives me of the opportunity to rejoice with the good fortune of another.

Whatever we are feeling at any given moment in life is an opportunity to learn and grow. This is really difficult to see when we are wrestling with some of the less desirable emotions such as anger, fear, or grief. Often the most intense emotions are our greatest teachers.

This process of sitting with feelings will not necessarily make them go away. It can, however, benefit our body, mind, and spirit. Acknowledging the feeling by attending to it will lessen the physical effects of the emotion on our body. We will become more accepting of the present moment. Either now, or in the future, we will become aware of the important psychological and spiritual lessons that this emotion is meant to teach us.

Reflection

Out of the night shadows
these deep, dark thoughts and feelings emerge
where they were hidden
all these years.
Like a frightened child
I want to run
but have no place to hide.
For how can one hide
from dreams larger than life
and feelings
that leave me crying in the dawn?

Do you presently feel some intense emotion? Try to sit
with the emotion in the presence of your spirit, and allow
it to speak to you. Think back over a time when you were
experiencing an intense feeling. Reflect on the influence
of that feeling on the situation. Does the situation look
different to you now?

27

Four A.M. Darkness

SOMETIMES I WAKE UP AT THREE-THIRTY OR FOUR IN THE MORNING with a feeling of fear and disorientation. Worries that I handled the day before with ease seem to have grown out of proportion. My fears loom larger than life, and it is not unusual to feel real terror deep inside. I know I am awake, and it is as if my worst nightmare has become a reality. With this experience comes a sense of hopelessness and an inability to cope.

If I get up and wander about my house, the usually familiar rooms seem to mirror my inner state of mind. Furniture takes on a strange, ghostlike appearance. Once-familiar surroundings contain shadows that were not there in the light of day.

I stumble around in the darkness until I remember that I am not alone. In my mind I head for the center of my being. As I enter my own inner room I am aware of the presence of the Holy One and the strength of my own spirit that will walk with me in the day to come. And so, at four in the morning, I sit quietly in the presence of the light, knowing that it will always be there for me.

Retirement and aging can bring shadows and ghosts that may haunt us—not only at four in the morning, but often in the light of day. Our fears can revolve around many issues in our lives. We may fear illness and a gradual decline in our physical strength. We worry about the happiness and well-being of our children, our grandchildren, and those we love. We may fear the loss of financial security, wondering whether we will outlive our resources. Our fears are often attached to things we cannot do anything about at the present moment. They are nonetheless real, and they disrupt our daily existence.

As I have pondered my own personal fears, in the presence of the Holy One, I have come to realize that I have very little control over any of my worries. I cannot see or prepare for every shadow that will fall across my life or the lives of those I love. I know one thing: I will not be alone in whatever dark places I will have to pass, and neither are my loved ones.

Our fears can be a thief, robbing us of joy, peace, happiness, and the beauty of the moment. Will we continue to spend time entertaining them, or will we let them go? Many of us would like to let our fears go, but don't know how.

I would like to suggest a few ideas that might help. As in all things, seek your own inner experience of the Holy. *Look within* to find your inner guide. *Ask* for help to let go of the fear. *Find a simple sentence* that you can repeat frequently during the day when fearful thoughts present themselves. Find words that feel comfortable to you, perhaps "I am not alone" or "God is with me." When we have a negative thought pattern, we need to retrain our thinking with repetition of a positive thought or affirmation.

Recently, I had cataract surgery. Was I fearful? You bet! If the anticipation of a surgeon cutting into my eye was not enough, my fears were rounded out nicely by reading the disclaimers of all that just might go wrong during the procedure.

I knew I needed to take action so my fears would not consume me. As I lay on the gurney, being prepared for surgery, I remembered that I was not alone. I chose this affirmation: "The love of God is flowing here." As I repeated this over and over again I asked a blessing on myself and all who were working with me. I extended that blessing to all the other patients waiting for surgery.

In addition to the words in my mind, I added a visual dimension. I "saw" with my mind's eye the light of God surrounding myself, the staff, and all the patients.

I could not dispel my fears completely, but through my spiritual resources I felt empowered to face whatever might come during this experience. As in most cases, the surgery was successful, and I have much clearer vision than before.

Each of us must walk through our own forest of fear during our lifetime. None of us walks alone. We all have spiritual resources. What a difference it makes in our lives when we know it.

Reflection

In the darkness
I walk through this forest of fear,
doubts, like small demons,
nipping at my heels
as my feet grope to find the unseen path.
Shadows trip me up
and in the moonless night
I battle with sadness.
Erie music floats from beyond
inviting me to a most macabre dance.
How long is this night?

Can you think of a time in your life when fear robbed you
of the joy of the moment? What are your present fears?
Prepare some affirmations and visualizations that are
meaningful to you and that you can use when you are
afraid. What can you say to yourself that will help you?

Now is the time to mourn the past
and embrace the promises of the future.

Now is the time to revisit our retirement dreams
and make them come true.

28

Measuring the Distance

RECENTLY, MY HUSBAND AND I WERE INVITED TO ATTEND THE Founder's Day celebration for the order of nuns where I had been a member for nineteen years. We knelt in that convent chapel, and my heart filled with intense joy as I looked around at the women who had been teachers, mothers, and sisters to me. I felt deep gratitude and love for all they had been to me during my years with them.

How different these feelings were from those I had held twenty-five years earlier, when I knelt in this same chapel preparing to sign papers that would separate me from the order. Then, I was anxious about the future. As I left the sheltering walls of the convent I was fearful about what lay ahead. I felt some anger and resentment toward the nuns for not being what I wanted them to be, for me.

Twenty-five years later, I can look back and see that they were exactly what they were meant to be. I know also that my time with them was meant to be temporary. Leaving was to be a part of my journey. I am at a point now where I can truly measure the distance and realize how far I have come.

Retirement gives each of us the opportunity to measure our own distance. Sometimes it takes an event, like the one described above, to juggle our minds into reflecting on the distance we have traveled. Perhaps you have had a similar experience at the wedding or graduation of your child. The birth of the first grandchild can also be a significant event that invites you to reflect on your life's journey.

As we re-walk our history, we gather the wisdom that we have gained over the years. We know that this review is a natural process as we grow older. We find ourselves recounting stories of our lives.

Recently I read in the *AARP Bulletin* that memoir writing has become very popular. Not long ago, I spoke to a friend who had just finished writing her memoirs, and she said she felt so much better about herself. She saw her failures, but she also became more in touch with her accomplishments and strengths.

Telling our stories to family and friends is a good way to begin our review. Writing down our memories is a great way to preserve our family history for future generations. Those special memories can be documented in photo albums or put on a tape recorder. Many people now are taking their old home movies and having them put on videotape.

The stories of our lives tell us who we are. They tell us where we have come from and what we have learned. Looking at the entire panorama of our lives, we come to new understandings about our journey. We come to appreciate all that we have endured, and we gather the wisdom we have learned for use now and in the future.

I often wondered why some people tell the same stories over and over again. Someone once told me that the story will continue to be told until an inner work has been accomplished, and then it will not be necessary to tell it any more.

As mentioned in chapter 6, "Soul Purpose," we had a particular reason in mind for coming to this earth. This purpose was clear to our spirit when we came. Our purpose in life will be clear to us after we have passed from the earth. We can better understand our life's purpose from the patterns we see emerging as we review our lives. We may see a certain situation happening often in our life. Our own spirit knows why this keeps happening, and it can guide us to a deeper understanding of the meaning of what we see in relation to our life goals.

Reviewing our lives in one form or another gives us the opportunity to better know who we are. As we look back over the years we realize that what we once thought of as failures have not devastated us. We can get in touch with our strengths and see how they have played out in our lives. We can become aware of unfinished business, knowing that there is still time to attend to it. We can gather the wisdom we have gained over the years and appreciate the person we have become.

Reflection

I walk along this once familiar road.
Memories lie scattered at my feet
all precious now
all with gifts to give.
What I once discarded
passing this way before
I pick up again and
in the light of the years now passed
I see a vein of gold
running through its center.

Various celebrations in our lives, such as weddings, births, funerals, or reunions, trigger remembrances of the past. What recent events in your life have invited you to look back on the past? Can you "measure the distance" and list strengths, skills, wisdom, and knowledge that have come from your journey?

Now is the time to look back over our lives and
appreciate the progress we have made.

Now is the time to make friends with
our feelings about retirement
and other issues in our lives.

29

Keeping in Step

I ALWAYS SMILE WHEN I HEAR THE STORY OF THE WOMAN WHO was watching a military parade. She remarked to her neighbor, "Look, everyone is out of step but my son, John!"

There are times in our post-retirement years when we feel useless and out of step with life. This is understandable, since the responsibilities of our working life set a rhythm to our days and weeks. We knew what day it was and what we had to do. Even though we did not always want to get up in the morning on work days, that morning ritual gave meaning and rhythm to our existence. Generally, we were able to see the value of what we did at work. Without that daily work pattern, we can feel floating and out of step.

Our culture has built a whole set of values around the work ethic—the drumbeat that kept us marching most of our lives. During our working years, we continued to ask such questions as these: "Am I getting paid what I am worth?" "Is there room for advancement in this work?" "What are my goals for the future?" While living in the present, we spent a lot of time and energy working toward the next step.

It seems that much of my own life has been that way. When I was in grade school I lived for high school. In high school, I looked forward to entering the convent. In training to become a religious sister, I looked forward to attending college. In college, I could hardly wait until I was teaching. While teaching, I looked forward to summer vacation. During the summer, I looked forward to starting the new school year. It seemed that what I was looking for was always just ahead. When I retired, it hit me: "What do I look forward to now?"

That question poses itself to every retiree, and we respond in different ways. Some of us will not listen to the question. Others try to continue marching to the drumbeat of work life, filling their days to the brim with volunteer and social activities. Yet, that gnawing question persists, and the only way to silence it is to answer it. At this point, it is time to look at the values by which we measure our existence now and in the days to come.

Sooner or later, we stop and realize that we are now marching to a different drummer. If we can be still long enough, we will hear the rhythm of a new drumbeat. Keeping in step with retirement and aging requires a whole different dance. For those who can hear the music, it is a rich and fulfilling experience.

What is really important to us now? It may be time to discover a new lifestyle—one that does not necessarily reflect the work ethic we lived by for so long. It may mean reexamining the values we have always held in a new light. If you are reading this book, you have begun the journey to redefining your lifestyle, and maybe some of your values, in this new stage of life.

As I look toward spirituality for answers, I reflect on these words of the esteemed rabbi Abraham Joshua Heschel:

"Just to be is a blessing, just to live is holy." My very presence on this planet is valuable for myself and for others. The love of the Holy continues to embrace me whether I am productive or not. My spiritual values tell me that where I am is where I need to be for my growth. If I am dissatisfied with where I am, I am robbing myself of the presence of the Holy that is always available.

This presence is actually found in the present moment, no matter how disconcerting or confusing that moment might seem. The more we are present to the moment, the more we immerse ourselves in the Holy. It is hard to be present to the moment if we do not value it. So many moments in our lives seem unimportant and even useless. We would rather be somewhere else, doing something else.

My own inner wisdom tells me that what I am looking for—what I have always looked for—has been right in front of me. The deepest peace and fulfillment wait in the present moment. Here we gather all the strands of our lives, incomplete as they may seem, and hold them as the most precious gift we could have at this time. They are just what we need to fulfill our purpose in life. This means that we embrace and value *all* the elements in this moment, especially the less desirable ones such as pain, uncertainty, confusion, depression, disappointment, and loss.

As we build some structure in our lives and see life from a spiritual perspective, we will find that our retirement years have a rhythm and meaning of their own that is deeply satisfying.

Reflection

This now will never be again.
We rush by this moment quickly
seeking life
yet fail to stop and embrace it
in this joy
this pain
this moment
this blessed now.

Are there times when you feel out of step with life? Do
you question the meaningfulness of what you do? Stop at
least once a day, and ask yourself this question: "Am I truly
present to this moment?" Recognize the presence of the
Holy in the present. Take time to recall the words of Rabbi
Heschel: "Just to be is a blessing, just to live is holy."

Now is the time to search the corners of our lives
for unfinished business, and finish it.

Now is the time to enter and relish
each moment we are given.

"Her Busy Day"

30

Getting the Job Done

HOW MANY OF OUR DAYS ARE SPENT JUST GETTING THE JOB done? Whether it is cleaning a room, writing a paper, or mowing the lawn, I look at the goal and then, with a kind of numb determination, plow through the work to its completion.

Recently I read a book by Thich Nhat Hanh called *The Miracle of Mindfulness*. It changed the way I looked at these repetitive and sometimes boring tasks. The initial challenge was to pay attention to each step in the process. In entering into the experience with our mind and all our senses, we become present to the moment. In entering into the moment, we enter the presence of the Holy.

This has to be experienced to be believed. I tried it the other day while weeding the vegetable garden. With lots of rain and warm weather, the weeds were flourishing, and my first feeling was discouragement as I thought, "It will take hours to pull all these weeds." I bent down and began to engage all of my senses in the work. I started to enjoy the process as I pulled each stem gently until I felt the roots releasing, and then gave a quick jerk and threw the weed into the bucket. In no time I had covered a square foot—and then another. My senses immersed themselves in the warm sunshine and cool breeze. The fragrance of lilacs floated from my neighbor's yard. The early morning quiet was broken only by the singing of the birds. I moved steadily across the garden in a somewhat euphoric state. I even felt sorry when there were no more weeds to pull. Did it take me hours? I don't really remember. I chalked up my pleasant experience to the fact that I really do like to garden.

But what about scrubbing kitchen cabinets? Now there is a challenge! I set upon this task with my usual "Let's get this job done" attitude, but then I remembered to enter into the experience. Sure enough, I found myself relishing the task. The smell of Murphy's Oil Soap and the squish of the rag led me into the activity. I enjoyed seeing the wood come to life as the dust and grime of the past year washed away.

Each day we perform many routine and not-so-routine tasks. They seem trivial and lacking in significance. They must be done before we can move on to the more important things in life.

Strange as it may seem, there is nothing more important than the bicycle we are fixing, the dish we are washing, or the snow we are shoveling. All can be doorways to the Divine Presence if we give them our full concentration and enter into them with focused attention.

Recently, I attended a wedding where the sister of the bride was profoundly challenged both physically and mentally. Even though she did not speak, she seemed to take in everything, and her bright smile and steady gaze conveyed a deep sense of delight in the present moment. Not wrapped in layers of sophistication, her spirit seemed to leap out and touch all with whom she came in contact. What a powerful teacher she was for me. This young woman showed me what it was to be totally present to the moment.

In our fast-paced world, many of us have established the habit of doing one thing and thinking about something else. We often try to do two things at once, while our attention jumps continually from one thing to the other.

To focus our attention on one activity sounds simple— and it is simple, but not easy. To do this, we need to allow all our mind and all our senses to be absorbed in the present activity. We must totally engage our sight, hearing, touch, smell, and taste in what we are doing. If we can do this, we may find peace and contentment in any task, no matter how small.

Reflection

Like a precious gift
I unwrap the present moment
carelessly tied
in newspaper and common twine.
Often I do not value what I see.
If only I could
pull aside
the human veil,
my spiritual eyes would see
it is the perfect gift
for now.

Certain activities we enjoy, or people we are with, can help us learn how to be present to the moment. What is it in your life that can totally engage you? Do you have a hobby in which you get lost? Is there someone you enjoy being with who makes you oblivious to the passage of time? In such situations, we are naturally focused on the moment. Observe those experiences, and apply that kind of concentration to other situations in your life. Start with simple, deliberate steps to change your way of doing things. Once you have experienced that sense of presence to the moment, you will find yourself seeking it more and more in the things you do.

31

Unfinished Business

WHEN I WAS A CHILD AND WE ATTENDED A CARNIVAL OR FAIR, the merry-go-round was my favorite activity. I always chose a horse that went up and down, looking with disdain upon those who sat in the little benches or who rode stationary horses. I waved to my parents as the merry-go-round started. As it began to move faster and faster my entire attention was focused on staying on the horse. I felt a shiver of fear as it seemed to be moving much higher than I thought it would. As I stole a glance at where I thought my parents were standing, the real world out there appeared a blur. The music, colors, and lights carried me into a world of enchantment as I perched on my steed. Fear and excitement mingled and left my adrenaline pumping. When the merry-go-round slowed, I felt both sadness and relief. I looked out into the real world to find my parents standing in the same place where I had left them.

When I entered into retirement, the experience of the merry-go-round came back to me. It seemed to mirror my life up to that point. Like the child who chose a horse, as a young person I made career choices that set in motion a whole experience of life. The momentum of my careers demanded a focus that left some aspects of life a blur.

Retirement is the slowing down of the merry-go-round. It is an opportunity to see and engage in life from a different point of view. In this slowing down, aspects of life that were once a blur become clearer. Some of that clarity falls on a category called unfinished business. This vast subject can refer to something as simple as sorting and filing old bills or to something as important as a relationship that needs mending. If we ask our inner wisdom to guide us, we will begin to see what is unfinished for us.

Most obvious in the unfinished business category are the material things. If I left the earth tomorrow, how would I want to leave things? What needs to be cleaned out or given away? Do I need a will or a trust? Do I want to make my final arrangements? These are no longer things that we can assign to a future time in life. There is no better time to do them than now, and we will be able to live the rest of our lives more peacefully and contentedly when we know that we have taken care of them.

Most important among unfinished business are relationships. Are there misunderstandings between ourselves and family members or friends? Are there things that I want, or need, to say to another that I have left unsaid? Retirement reminds me that I do not have forever.

Taking care of business is more than attending to our material affairs and relationships. Maybe we have had a dream all our lives. That dream might be to travel, write a book, paint with oils, or knit a sweater. There are many stories of retirees who have pursued their dreams. Recently we attended a book-signing by an eighty-four-year-old woman who, during her retirement, had biked all over the world and then had written about it. We often hear of retirees who have gone on to fulfill their dreams, but I wonder how many have let their dreams die with them.

When I went to visit my grandmother as a child, I observed certain spiritual practices that were part of her life. At various times during the day she could be seen with her well-worn prayer book, communicating with God. She often walked the mile or so to the neighborhood church for Mass during the week. There she joined a group of older folks in daily worship. I began to believe that one of the tasks of aging was to develop a closer relationship with God.

Perhaps your relationship with the Holy in your life is an item of unfinished business on your list. You may want to explore the spirituality I have outlined in the first two parts of this book, or you may want to examine, in more depth, your own religious tradition.

Even though our professional life has ended, we all realize that we have unfinished personal business. Recognizing and accomplishing these tasks will bring a sense of peace into our retirement years.

Reflection

The edges
of the old afghan
have come unraveled.
This special blanket
has warmed and comforted my soul
in joy and sorrow
all my life.
Now I must attend to it
and with loving hand
untangle the threads and
gather the strands together
knitting together the torn places
so that it may cover me well
when I am old.

Take some time to review your finances, your relationships with others and God, and the hopes and dreams
that have been with you for a lifetime. Can you find
unfinished business in any areas of your life? Make a list
of those things you would like to accomplish before you
leave this earth.

32

Four Steps to a Better Day

THE THOUGHTS WE HAVE ON AWAKENING ARE SOME OF THE MOST important of the day. They will often set the tone and direction for the rest of the day. We can make a conscious decision to choose thoughts that will align our day with our deepest purpose in life. Here are four statements that can help direct your day. When you awaken, and before you get out of bed, take a few minutes to reflect on them in view of your own life.

1. I am a spiritual being having a human experience.
   I align my body, mind, will, and emotions with my
   spiritual center and the God within.

It is possible that most of us have days when we awaken feeling afraid, worried, or overwhelmed by what we know must be done that day. We tend to get absorbed in the feelings of the moment. In the midst of all this, we are very aware of our human experience but have forgotten that we are also spiritual beings. Remembering that I am a spiritual being and aligning all my human concerns with that inner wisdom puts my life in perspective. As I recall that I existed before I came to this earth, and that I will exist after I leave this earth, I refocus my vision on the big picture.

2. I have come to this earth for a spiritual purpose.
From the time we are young, we are taught to set goals relating to all areas of our lives. We spend our lives pursuing these goals pertaining to family, academic achievement, careers, and personal wealth. Retirement is a time when all of us tend to look back over the goals we have had in our lifetime. We are inclined to judge ourselves by the way in which we did or did not achieve these goals. Most retirees will express regrets for goals not achieved. The money we did not make, the position we did not attain, the failure of a marriage all leave room for regrets.

In addition to the material goals mentioned above, I had definite spiritual goals in mind when I made the decision to come to this earth. I came for the purpose of accomplishing these goals, my soul purpose. I asked that my life unfold in such a way that my spiritual goals would be accomplished. While I do not remember these decisions, my soul purpose is written deep within my spirit, and my spirit continues to guide me daily in accomplishing these goals.

When I recall on awakening each morning that I have a spiritual purpose, I begin to re-vision my life—not just in the light of my human goals, which are well and good, but in the light of the bigger picture. Some of my most cherished human goals have not been accomplished. I do not see that as a failure but as a sign that they were not meant to be in light of the big picture. Led by my inner wisdom, I know that my soul purpose has been, and continues to be, accomplished now and until the end of my life. The wonderful thing about soul purpose is that nothing can stand in the way of its accomplishment. Neither old age, sickness, handicaps, poverty, nor even mental illness can stand in the way of my soul purpose, which continues to unfold every day of my life upon this earth.

3. Today I will live in the present moment, knowing that I have all I need to accomplish my real purpose in life.

Life is lived in the present moment. Even though I know this, I tend to spend a lot of present moments worrying about the future or regretting the past. That is why it is so important for me to remind myself of this each morning. When we stay in the present moment, we trust the Holy in our lives to watch over us and provide for our daily needs. The catch is, of course, that we will be provided with what we *truly* need, not what we *think* we need.

4. I count my blessings.

There is no better way to launch the day than with a heart grateful to the Holy for all the blessings we have in our lives. For each of us, this expression will be different. Sometimes I reflect on something specific that happened the day before: the kindness of a stranger who helped me pick up groceries spilled from a broken bag, the cheerfulness of the clerk, or the driver who stopped to let me into a line of traffic.

Often I try to think about blessings that I take for granted: a warm house on a winter day, food on the table, the companionship of my family. With only a little probing, my mind is deluged with those gifts usually taken for granted. I am reminded that everything is a gift, including my very existence.

If you choose to begin your day with these four steps, remember that what is important is not the wording of the statement but the thought. You will find after a while that you no longer need the words. The thought simply comes to you, and the four ideas move smoothly through your mind.

Visualization has been an important part of my awakening ritual. I visualize my spirit as a bright light. I see my body centered in the midst of this light. From this picture in my mind, these steps seem to flow naturally. Each of us must find the way that works best for us. Ask your own inner wisdom to be your guide.

Reflection

Morning dawns
and light surrounds me.
I reach out and pull my body, mind, and will
into the circle of light.
It is in this place
that I am renewed
and find direction for the day.
In all the roads I travel today,
I will remember the invisible light
that walks with me.

What are your first thoughts when you awaken in the morning? Do you find them influencing your day? If your waking moments are not helping you to a better day, you may wish to recall on awakening that you are a spiritual being who has come to this earth for a special purpose. You may not understand that purpose, but it is written deep within you, and your spirit understands. Ask that your mind, body, will, and emotions be in line with your spiritual purpose, and know that you have everything you need in the present moment to accomplish that purpose.

33

Going Home

MY HUSBAND AND I LOVE TO TRAVEL. PROBABLY OUR GREATEST travel adventure occurred when we went to Alaska. One sunny summer day we left Columbus, Ohio, with camper in tow, bound for the great wilderness. Even though we had read the travel books and seen the videos, nothing could have prepared us for the adventure that was about to unfold. Little did we realize how arduous it would be to drive forty-three hundred miles to reach our destination. As we traveled through parts of Yukon Territory in Canada, it was not unusual to drive for hours without seeing another human being. Without TV, radio, or newspapers, we were left wondering what was happening in the rest of the world. Sometimes the trip seemed lonely, and we learned to depend on each other and our dog for companionship.

Nothing could compare with the sense of wilderness that we experienced during these times. Beauty met us at every turn. The road carried us through forests of fir trees and past the blue-green waters of Lake Kluane. In Denali Park we were dazzled with the beauty of Mt. McKinley emerging from the clouds.

Our adventure held excitement and challenge, but in the midst of it, there were times when I was homesick for our little brick ranch home and would have given anything to be sitting in our family room, reading the newspaper. We had never been so far away from home, or stayed so long. Six weeks away seemed like an eternity. Needless to say, nothing could compare with the feeling I had when we completed our round trip of more than nine thousand miles and drove up in front of our house in Columbus, Ohio. We were home.

We greeted our neighbors and called friends and relatives we had not seen for a long time. We carefully inspected the house inside and out. Some of my garden plants had grown so tall that I hardly recognized them. The feeders were empty, and the birds had disappeared from our yard. There was a lot to do, but it was so good to be home again and to see and touch all those familiar things that had become dear to us.

Going home, for me, means going back to what is familiar. These rooms and windows hold memories of the past and dreams for the future. This is the place where I am most myself. After our many trips, it is the place to which I return, to take up the strands of my life and be renewed.

Death is going home. What may surprise us is that it is coming home to a familiar place. We know this place. We have been here before. Not only do we know it, we love it. Stored here are memories of past lives and hopes for future growth. Here we establish contact with friends and relatives that have passed on. Here we review our life, without judgment, and make plans for the future.

Our culture is filled with many fears and misconceptions about death. Probably the greatest of these is denial—a denial that refuses to talk about the experience. We spend a great deal of time and money negating the existence of death.

Funeral directors work to make the dead body appear just as it was in life. When they view the casket, relatives and friends talk about how "good" the deceased looks.

In reality, the body is clothing for the spirit. When we take off our winter coat or discard clothing that no longer fits, are we still the same person? Our spiritual beliefs tell us that our body is the destructible clothing for our spirit. When we discard it, we are still the same being. Nothing essential to who we really are is lost.

Recently I dreamed that I was standing beside the bed of an older woman who had died of cancer. I looked down and noticed that she had written a letter of instructions to her relatives. Then, looking more closely at the woman, I realized that she was me! My first thought was, "Oh, my gosh, I am dead. That really went fast." It was hard to believe that I was dead because I felt just like myself. My second thought was, "I am so glad I wrote those instructions to my relatives, because I have no way of communicating with them now." Then I woke up. I truly believe that this dream was given to me to help me understand that I will still be myself after I die.

Other dreams have provided me with deeper spiritual insights about death, such as the following one: My husband and I are in our van, waiting at multiple tracks for two trains to pass. After they pass we start across the tracks. At midpoint I see the same two trains backing up. They are approaching our van at a high speed. I know we will be hit. In an instant I feel the impact and deep sadness as I think about being separated from Bernie. I wait for the pain, but it does not come. I wonder: will we survive this?

I wake up. My heart is pounding. I reach out to touch Bernie, who is quietly sleeping next to me. The experience was so real that it takes me a few minutes to realize that I was dreaming. This dream stays with me all day.

I think the experience of death is like waking up from a dream. Just as I wake up from a dream in sleep, death is a waking up to another world, one with a greater dimension of reality than I could have imagined.

The spiritual beliefs presented in this book can lead us to a deeper understanding of death. Death is a passage to another phase of life. We continue to be who we are as we make this transition. We go to a place that is familiar, and we are greeted by family and friends who have gone before us. In death we know that we are truly home.

Reflection

I pause along life's journey
and look back
to see from where I've come.
The road behind me
reveals a rich tapestry of pain and joy
backed by the sameness of each day's living.
Now I look ahead
and through the mist that blankets the road
the eyes of my spirit
see a door through which I will someday pass.
I believe it is a friendly door.
As I pass through this door
I see the smile of loved ones
who went ahead of me.
I walk down streets made familiar
with all the things I thought I left behind,
and I know that I am truly home.

Imagine that you stand at the door of death. What do you
believe is beyond the door? Where did your beliefs come
from: society? your family? your religion? Allow the light
of your spirit to shine on your experience. In the light of
your spirit, does your experience change?

34

Now Is the Time

WHEN WE WERE YOUNGER, TIME WAS ON OUR SIDE—OR SO WE thought. There was always time in the years ahead to accomplish some cherished project. Our hopes and dreams were assigned to the future, with a promise to ourselves and others that eventually we would achieve them. When we retire, we are faced with the fact that our future is now. No more can we assign our expectations to the future. It is now or never.

Now is the time to stop and reflect.
Now is the time to reach inward and touch our essence.
Now is the time to strip away the many faces of the roles we have played, and recognize who we really are.
Now is the time to understand that we are spiritual beings having a human experience.
Now is the time to perceive our spiritual dimension—the strong, silent presence of our spirit.
Now is the time to reflect on our lives and recognize the strength of spirit that has been there.
Now is the time to acknowledge that our purpose on this earth is a spiritual one, and was determined before we came here.

Now is the time to listen to the daily inner whisperings of
    our spirit.
Now is the time to identify who God has been for us in
    the past.
Now is the time to find out who God is for us now.
Now is the time to mourn the past and embrace the promises
    of the future.
Now is the time to revisit our retirement dreams and make
    them come true.
Now is the time to look deep within ourselves and refocus
    our energies on the goals that are most important to us.
Now is the time to love and appreciate ourselves and others
    in a new light.
Now is the time to look back over our lives and appreciate
    the progress we have made.
Now is the time to make friends with our feelings about
    retirement and other issues in our lives.
Now is the time to search the corners of our lives for
    unfinished business, and finish it.
Now is the time to look toward death with acceptance,
    knowing it is just another door in the progression of
    our existence.
Now is the time to enter and relish each moment we
    are given.

ABOUT THE AUTHOR

Molly Srode is a retired hospital chaplain in her early sixties. A spiritual seeker, Molly easily shares details of her own spiritual journey (she was once a Catholic nun and educator) with readers of all faith traditions. She and her husband, Bernie, have been actively pursuing their spiritual lives together over the past twenty-five years. They are publishers of the *Senior Spirituality Newsletter,* and live in Columbus, Ohio.

Notes

Notes

Notes

Notes

Notes

About SKYLIGHT PATHS Publishing

SkyLight Paths Publishing is creating a place where people of different spiritual traditions come together for challenge and inspiration, a place where we can help each other understand the mystery that lies at the heart of our existence.

Through spirituality, our religious beliefs are increasingly becoming a part of our lives—rather than *apart* from our lives. While many of us may be more interested than ever in spiritual growth, we may be less firmly planted in traditional religion. Yet, we do want to deepen our relationship to the sacred, to learn from our own as well as from other faith traditions, and to practice in new ways.

SkyLight Paths sees both believers and seekers as a community that increasingly transcends traditional boundaries of religion and denomination—people wanting to learn from each other, *walking together, finding the way.*

We at SkyLight Paths take great care to produce beautiful books that present meaningful spiritual content in a form that reflects the art of making high quality books. Therefore, we want to acknowledge those who contributed to the production of this book.

PRODUCTION
Sara Dismukes, Tim Holtz,
Martha McKinney & Bridgett Taylor

EDITORIAL
Rebecca Castellano, Amanda Dupuis, Polly Short Mahoney,
Lauren Seidman, Maura D. Shaw & Emily Wichland

COVER DESIGN
Bridgett Taylor

TEXT DESIGN
Susan Ramundo, SR Desktop Services, Ridge, New York

PRINTING & BINDING
Lake Book, Melrose Park, Illinois

Other Interesting Books—Spirituality

Lighting the Lamp of Wisdom: *A Week Inside a Yoga Ashram*
by *John Ittner;* Foreword by *Dr. David Frawley*

This insider's guide to Hindu spiritual life takes you into a typical week of retreat inside a yoga ashram to demystify the experience and show you what to expect from your own visit. Includes a discussion of worship services, meditation and yoga classes, chanting and music, work practice, and more.

6 x 9, 192 pp, b/w photographs, Quality PB, ISBN 1-893361-52-7 **$15.95**; HC, ISBN 1-893361-37-3 **$24.95**

Waking Up: *A Week Inside a Zen Monastery*
by *Jack Maguire;* Foreword by *John Daido Loori, Roshi*

An essential guide to what it's like to spend a week inside a Zen Buddhist monastery.

6 x 9, 224 pp, b/w photographs, HC, ISBN 1-893361-13-6 **$21.95**

Making a Heart for God: *A Week Inside a Catholic Monastery*
by *Dianne Aprile;* Foreword by *Brother Patrick Hart,* OCSO

This essential guide to experiencing life in a Catholic monastery takes you to the Abbey of Gethsemani—the Trappist monastery in Kentucky that was home to author Thomas Merton—to explore the details. "More balanced and informative than the popular *The Cloister Walk* by Kathleen Norris." —*Choice: Current Reviews for Academic Libraries*

6 x 9, 224 pp, b/w photographs, Quality PB, ISBN 1-893361-49-7 **$16.95**; HC, ISBN 1-893361-14-4 **$21.95**

Come and Sit: *A Week Inside Meditation Centers*
by *Marcia Z. Nelson;* Foreword by *Wayne Teasdale*

The insider's guide to meditation in a variety of different spiritual traditions. Traveling through Buddhist, Hindu, Christian, Jewish, and Sufi traditions, this essential guide takes you to different meditation centers to meet the teachers and students and learn about the practices, demystifying the meditation experience.

6 x 9, 224 pp, b/w photographs, Quality PB, ISBN 1-893361-35-7 **$16.95**

Or phone, fax, mail or e-mail to: SKYLIGHT PATHS Publishing
Sunset Farm Offices, Route 4 • P.O. Box 237 • Woodstock, Vermont 05091
Tel: (802) 457-4000   Fax: (802) 457-4004   www.skylightpaths.com
Credit card orders: (800) 962-4544 (8:30AM–5:30PM ET Monday–Friday)
Generous discounts on quantity orders. SATISFACTION GUARANTEED. Prices subject to change.

Spirituality

Who Is My God?
An Innovative Guide to Finding Your Spiritual Identity
Created by *the Editors at SkyLight Paths*

Spiritual Type™ + Tradition Indicator = Spiritual Identity

Your Spiritual Identity is an undeniable part of who you are—whether you've thought much about it or not. This dynamic resource provides a helpful framework to begin or deepen your spiritual growth. Start by taking the unique Spiritual Identity Self-Test™; tabulate your results; then explore one, two, or more of twenty-eight faiths/spiritual paths followed in America today. "An innovative and entertaining way to think—and rethink—about your own spiritual path, or perhaps even to find one." —Dan Wakefield, author of *How Do We Know When It's God?*
6 x 9, 160 pp, Quality PB, ISBN 1-893361-08-X **$15.95**

Spiritual Manifestos: *Visions for Renewed Religious Life in America from Young Spiritual Leaders of Many Faiths*
Edited by *Niles Elliot Goldstein;* Preface by *Martin E. Marty*

Discover the reasons why so many people have kept organized religion at arm's length.

Here, ten young spiritual leaders, most in their mid-thirties, representing the spectrum of religious traditions—Protestant, Catholic, Jewish, Buddhist, Unitarian Universalist—present the innovative ways they are transforming our spiritual communities and our lives. "These ten articulate young spiritual leaders engender hope for the vitality of 21st-century religion." —Forrest Church, Minister of All Souls Church in New York City
6 x 9, 256 pp, HC, ISBN 1-893361-09-8 **$21.95**

  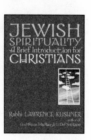 

Jewish Spirituality: *A Brief Introduction for Christians*
by *Lawrence Kushner*

Lawrence Kushner, whose award-winning books have brought Jewish spirituality to life for countless readers of all faiths and backgrounds, tailors his unique style to address Christians' questions, revealing the essence of Judaism in a way that people whose own tradition traces its roots to Judaism can understand and enjoy.
5½ x 8½, 112 pp, Quality PB, ISBN 1-58023-150-0 **$12.95**

The Geography of Faith
Underground Conversations on Religious, Political and Social Change
by *Daniel Berrigan* and *Robert Coles;* Updated introduction and afterword by the authors

A classic of faith-based activism—updated for a new generation.

Listen in on the conversations between these two great teachers—one a renegade priest wanted by the FBI for his protests against the Vietnam war, the other a future Pulitzer Prize-winning journalist—as they struggle with what it means to put your faith to the test. Discover how their story of challenging the status quo during a time of great political, religious, and social change is just as applicable to our lives today. 6 x 9, 224 pp, Quality PB, ISBN 1-893361-40-3 **$16.95**

Spiritual Biography

The Life of Evelyn Underhill
An Intimate Portrait of the Groundbreaking Author of Mysticism
by *Margaret Cropper;* Foreword by *Dana Greene*

Evelyn Underhill was a passionate writer and teacher who wrote elegantly on mysticism, worship, and devotional life. This is the story of how she made her way toward spiritual maturity, from her early days of agnosticism to the years when her influence was felt throughout the world. 6 x 9, 288 pp, 5 b/w photos, Quality PB, ISBN 1-893361-70-5 **$18.95**

Zen Effects: *The Life of Alan Watts*
by *Monica Furlong*

The first and only full-length biography of one of the most charismatic spiritual leaders of the twentieth century—now back in print!

Through his widely popular books and lectures, Alan Watts (1915–1973) did more to introduce Eastern philosophy and religion to Western minds than any figure before or since. Here is the only biography of this charismatic figure, who served as Zen teacher, Anglican priest, lecturer, academic, entertainer, a leader of the San Francisco renaissance, and author of more than 30 books, including *The Way of Zen, Psychotherapy East and West* and *The Spirit of Zen.* 6 x 9, 264 pp, Quality PB, ISBN 1-893361-32-2 **$16.95**

  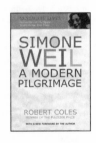 

Simone Weil: *A Modern Pilgrimage*
by *Robert Coles*

The extraordinary life of the spiritual philosopher who's been called both saint and madwoman.

The French writer and philosopher Simone Weil (1906–1943) devoted her life to a search for God—while avoiding membership in organized religion. Robert Coles' intriguing study of Weil details her short, eventful life, and is an insightful portrait of the beloved and controversial thinker whose life and writings influenced many (from T. S. Eliot to Adrienne Rich to Albert Camus), and continue to inspire seekers everywhere. 6 x 9, 208 pp, Quality PB, ISBN 1-893361-34-9 **$16.95**

Inspired Lives: *Exploring the Role of Faith and Spirituality in the Lives of Extraordinary People*
by *Joanna Laufer* and *Kenneth S. Lewis*

Contributors include *Ang Lee, Wynton Marsalis, Kathleen Norris, Hakeem Olajuwon, Christopher Parkening, Madeleine L'Engle, Doc Watson,* and many more

In this moving book, soul-searching conversations unearth the importance of spirituality and personal faith for more than forty artists and innovators who have made a real difference in our world through their work. 6 x 9, 256 pp, Quality PB, ISBN 1-893361-33-0 **$16.95**

Spiritual Practice

Women Pray
Voices through the Ages, from Many Faiths, Cultures, and Traditions
Edited and with introductions by *Monica Furlong*

Many ways—new and old—to communicate with the Divine.

This beautiful gift book celebrates the rich variety of ways women around the world have called out to the Divine—with words of joy, praise, gratitude, wonder, petition, longing, and even anger—from the ancient world up to our own time. Prayers from women of nearly every religious or spiritual background give us an eloquent expression of what it means to communicate with God. 5 x7¼,256 pp, Deluxe HC with ribbon marker, ISBN 1-893361-25-X **$19.95**

Praying with Our Hands: *Twenty-One Practices of Embodied Prayer from the World's Spiritual Traditions*
by *Jon M. Sweeney*; Photographs by *Jennifer J. Wilson*;
Foreword by *Mother Tessa Bielecki*; Afterword by *Taitetsu Unno, Ph.D.*

A spiritual guidebook for bringing prayer into our bodies.

This inspiring book of reflections and accompanying photographs shows us twenty-one simple ways of using our hands to speak to God, to enrich our devotion and ritual. All express the various approaches of the world's religious traditions to bringing the body into worship. Spiritual traditions represented include Anglican, Sufi, Zen, Roman Catholic, Yoga, Shaker, Hindu, Jewish, Pentecostal, Eastern Orthodox, and many others.
8 x 8, 96 pp, 22 duotone photographs, Quality PB, ISBN 1-893361-16-0 **$16.95**

  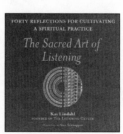 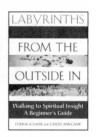

The Sacred Art of Listening
Forty Reflections for Cultivating a Spiritual Practice
by *Kay Lindahl*; Illustrations by *Amy Schnapper*

More than ever before, we need to embrace the skills and practice of listening. You will learn to: Speak clearly from your heart • Communicate with courage and compassion • Heighten your awareness for deep listening • Enhance your ability to listen to people with different belief systems. 8 x 8, 160 pp, Illus., Quality PB, ISBN 1-893361-44-6 **$16.95**

Labyrinths from the Outside In
Walking to Spiritual Insight—a Beginner's Guide
by *Donna Schaper* and *Carole Ann Camp*

The user-friendly, interfaith guide to making and using labyrinths— for meditation, prayer, and celebration.

Labyrinth walking is a spiritual exercise *anyone* can do. This accessible guide unlocks the mysteries of the labyrinth for all of us, providing ideas for using the labyrinth walk for prayer, meditation, and celebrations to mark the most important moments in life. Includes instructions for making a labyrinth of your own and finding one in your area.
6 x 9, 208 pp, b/w illus. and photographs, Quality PB, ISBN 1-893361-18-7 **$16.95**

SkyLight Illuminations Series
Andrew Harvey, series editor

Offers today's spiritual seeker an enjoyable entry into the great classic texts of the world's spiritual traditions. Each classic is presented in an accessible translation, with facing pages of guided commentary from experts, giving you the keys you need to understand the history, context, and meaning of the text. This series enables readers of all backgrounds to experience and understand classic spiritual texts directly, and to make them a part of their lives. Andrew Harvey writes the foreword to each volume, an insightful, personal introduction to each classic.

Bhagavad Gita: *Annotated & Explained*
Translation by *Shri Purohit Swami;* Annotation by *Kendra Crossen Burroughs*

"The very best Gita for first-time readers." —Ken Wilber

Millions of people turn daily to India's most beloved holy book, whose universal appeal has made it popular with non-Hindus and Hindus alike. This edition introduces you to the characters; explains references and philosophical terms; shares the interpretations of famous spiritual leaders and scholars; and more. 5½ x 8½, 192 pp, Quality PB, ISBN 1-893361-28-4 **$16.95**

  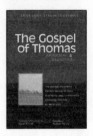

The Way of a Pilgrim: *Annotated & Explained*
Translation and annotation by *Gleb Pokrovsky*

The classic of Russian spirituality—now with facing-page commentary that illuminates and explains the text for you.

This delightful account is the story of one man who sets out to learn the prayer of the heart—also known as the "Jesus prayer"—and how the practice transforms his existence. This edition guides you through an abridged version of the text with facing-page annotations explaining the names, terms and references. 5½ x 8½, 160 pp, Quality PB, ISBN 1-893361-31-4 **$14.95**

The Gospel of Thomas: *Annotated & Explained*
Translation and annotation by *Stevan Davies*

The recently discovered mystical sayings of Jesus—now with facing-page commentary that illuminates and explains the text for you.

Discovered in 1945, this collection of aphoristic sayings sheds new light on the origins of Christianity and the intriguing figure of Jesus, portraying the Kingdom of God as a present fact about the world, rather than a future promise or future threat. This edition guides you through the text with annotations that focus on the meaning of the sayings, ideal for readers with no previous background in Christian history or thought.
5½ x 8½, 192 pp, Quality PB, ISBN 1-893361-45-4 **$15.95**

SkyLight Illuminations Series
Andrew Harvey, series editor

Zohar: *Annotated & Explained*
Translation and annotation by *Daniel C. Matt*

The cornerstone text of Kabbalah, now with facing-page commentary that illuminates and explains the text for you.

The best-selling author of *The Essential Kabbalah* brings together in one place the most important teachings of the *Zohar*, the canonical text of Jewish mystical tradition. Guides readers step by step through the midrash, mystical fantasy and Hebrew scripture that make up the *Zohar*, explaining the inner meanings in facing-page commentary. Ideal for readers without any prior knowledge of Jewish mysticism.
5½ x 8½, 176 pp, Quality PB, ISBN 1-893361-51-9 **$15.95**

 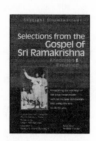 

Selections from the Gospel of Sri Ramakrishna
Annotated & Explained
Translation by *Swami Nikhilananda*; Annotation by *Kendra Crossen Burroughs*

The words of India's greatest example of God-consciousness and mystical ecstasy in recent history—now with facing-page commentary that illuminates and explains the text for you.

Introduces the fascinating world of the Indian mystic and the universal appeal of his message that has inspired millions of devotees for more than a century. Selections from the original text and insightful yet unobtrusive commentary highlight the most important and inspirational teachings. Ideal for readers without any prior knowledge of Hinduism.
5½ x 8½, 240 pp, b/w photographs, Quality PB, ISBN 1-893361-46-2 **$16.95**

Dhammapada: *Annotated & Explained*
Translation by *Max Müller*; Annotation by *Jack Maguire*

The classic of Buddhist spiritual practice—now with facing-page commentary that illuminates and explains the text for you.

The Dhammapada—words spoken by the Buddha himself over 2,500 years ago—is notoriously difficult to understand for the first-time reader. Now you can experience it with understanding even if you have no previous knowledge of Buddhism. Enlightening facing-page commentary explains all the names, terms, and references, giving you deeper insight into the text. An excellent introduction to Buddhist life and practice.
5½ x 8½, 160 pp, Quality PB, ISBN 1-893361-42-X **$14.95**

Meditation/Prayer

Finding Grace at the Center: *The Beginning of Centering Prayer*
by M. Basil Pennington, OCSO, Thomas Keating, OCSO, and Thomas E. Clarke, SJ

The book that helped launch the Centering Prayer "movement." Explains the prayer of *The Cloud of Unknowing*, posture and relaxation, the three simple rules of centering prayer, and how to cultivate centering prayer throughout all aspects of your life.
5 x 7¼,112 pp, HC, ISBN 1-893361-69-1 **$14.95**

Three Gates to Meditation Practice
A Personal Journey into Sufism, Buddhism, and Judaism
by David A. Cooper

Shows us how practicing within more than one spiritual tradition can lead us to our true home.

Here are over fifteen years from the journey of "post-denominational rabbi" David A. Cooper, author of *God Is a Verb*, and his wife, Shoshana—years in which the Coopers explored a rich variety of practices, from chanting Sufi *dhikr* to Buddhist Vipassanā meditation, to the study of Kabbalah and esoteric Judaism. Their experience demonstrates that the spiritual path is really completely within our reach, whoever we are, whatever we do—as long as we are willing to practice it. 5½ x 8½, 240 pp, Quality PB, ISBN 1-893361-22-5 **$16.95**

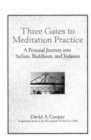

Silence, Simplicity & Solitude
A Complete Guide to Spiritual Retreat at Home
by David A. Cooper

The classic personal spiritual retreat guide that enables readers to create their own self-guided spiritual retreat at home.

Award-winning author David Cooper traces personal mystical retreat in all of the world's major traditions, describing the varieties of spiritual practices for modern spiritual seekers. Cooper shares the techniques and practices that encompass the personal spiritual retreat experience, allowing readers to enhance their meditation practices and create an effective, self-guided spiritual retreat in their own homes—without the instruction of a meditation teacher. 5½ x 8½, 336 pp, Quality PB, ISBN 1-893361-04-7 **$16.95**

Prayer for People Who Think Too Much
A Guide to Everyday, Anywhere Prayer from the World's Faith Traditions
by Mitch Finley

Helps us make prayer a natural part of daily living.

Takes a thoughtful look at how each major faith tradition incorporates prayer into *daily* life. Explores Christian sacraments, Jewish holy days, Muslim daily prayer, "mindfulness" in Buddhism, and more, to help you better understand and enhance your own prayer practices. "I love this book." —Caroline Myss, author of *Anatomy of the Spirit*
5½ x 8½, 224 pp, Quality PB, ISBN 1-893361-21-7 **$16.95**; HC, ISBN 1-893361-00-4 **$21.95**

Spirituality

A Heart of Stillness
A Complete Guide to Learning the Art of Meditation
by *David A. Cooper*

The only complete, nonsectarian guide to meditation, from one of our most respected spiritual teachers.

Experience what mystics have experienced for thousands of years. *A Heart of Stillness* helps you acquire on your own, with minimal guidance, the skills of various styles of meditation. Draws upon the wisdom teachings of Christianity, Judaism, Buddhism, Hinduism, and Islam as it teaches you the processes of purification, concentration, and mastery in detail.
5½ x 8½, 272 pp, Quality PB, ISBN 1-893361-03-9 **$16.95**

Silence, Simplicity & Solitude
A Complete Guide to Spiritual Retreat at Home
by *David A. Cooper*

The classic personal spiritual retreat guide that enables readers to create their own self-guided spiritual retreat at home.

Award-winning author David Cooper traces personal mystical retreat in all of the world's major traditions, describing the varieties of spiritual practices for modern spiritual seekers. Cooper shares the techniques and practices that encompass the personal spiritual retreat experience, allowing readers to enhance their meditation practices and create an effective, self-guided spiritual retreat in their own homes—without the instruction of a meditation teacher. 5½ x 8½, 336 pp, Quality PB, ISBN 1-893361-04-7 **$16.95**

  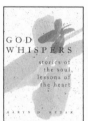 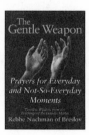 

God Whispers: *Stories of the Soul, Lessons of the Heart*
by Rabbi Karyn D. Kedar 6 x 9, 176 pp, Quality PB, ISBN 1-58023-088-1 **$15.95**

The Empty Chair: *Finding Hope and Joy—*
Timeless Wisdom from a Hasidic Master, Rebbe Nachman of Breslov AWARD WINNER!
Adapted by Moshe Mykoff and the Breslov Research Institute
4 x 6, 128 pp, Deluxe PB, 2-color text, ISBN 1-879045-67-2 **$9.95**

The Gentle Weapon: *Prayers for Everyday and Not-So-Everyday Moments*
Adapted from the Wisdom of Rebbe Nachman of Breslov by Moshe Mykoff and
S. C. Mizrahi, with the Breslov Research Institute
4 x 6, 144 pp, Deluxe PB, 2-color text, ISBN 1-58023-022-9 **$9.95**

Children's Spirituality

Becoming Me: *A Story of Creation*
by *Martin Boroson*

For ages 4 & up

Full-color illus. by *Christopher Gilvan-Cartwright*

Told in the personal "voice" of the Creator, here is a story about creation and relationship that is about each one of us. In simple words and with radiant illustrations, the Creator tells an intimate story about love, about friendship and playing, about our world—and about ourselves. And with each turn of the page, we're reminded that we just might be closer to our Creator than we think!

8 x 10, 32 pp, Full-color illus., HC, ISBN 1-893361-11-X **$16.95**

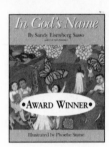

A Prayer for the Earth
The Story of Naamah, Noah's Wife
by *Sandy Eisenberg Sasso*
Full-color illus. by *Bethanne Andersen*

For ages 4 & up

This new story, based on an ancient text, opens readers' religious imaginations to new ideas about the well-known story of the Flood. When God tells Noah to bring the animals of the world onto the ark, God also calls on Naamah, Noah's wife, to save each plant on Earth. "A lovely tale.... Children of all ages should be drawn to this parable for our times."
—Tomie de Paola, artist/author of books for children
9 x 12, 32 pp, HC, Full-color illus., ISBN 1-879045-60-5 **$16.95**

In God's Name
by *Sandy Eisenberg Sasso*; Full-color illus. by *Phoebe Stone*

For ages 4 & up

Like an ancient myth in its poetic text and vibrant illustrations, this award-winning modern fable about the search for God's name celebrates the diversity and, at the same time, the unity of all the people of the world.
9 x 12, 32 pp, HC, Full-color illus., ISBN 1-879045-26-5 **$16.95**

Also available in Spanish:
El nombre de Dios 9 x 12, 32 pp, HC, Full-color illus., ISBN 1-893361-63-2 **$16.95**

The 11th Commandment
Wisdom from Our Children
by *The Children of America*

For ages 4 & up

"If there were an Eleventh Commandment, what would it be?" Children of many religious denominations across America answer this question—in their own drawings and words. "A rare book of spiritual celebration for all people, of all ages, for all time." —*Bookviews*
8 x 10, 48 pp, HC, Full-color illus., ISBN 1-879045-46-X **$16.95**

Children's Spirituality

God Said Amen

by *Sandy Eisenberg Sasso*
Full-color illus. by *Avi Katz*

> For ages 4 & up

A warm and inspiring tale of two kingdoms: Midnight Kingdom is overflowing with water but has no oil to light its lamps; Desert Kingdom is blessed with oil but has no water to grow its gardens. The kingdoms' rulers ask God for help but are too stubborn to ask each other. It takes a minstrel, a pair of royal riding-birds and their young keepers, and a simple act of kindness to show that they need only reach out to each other to find the answers to their prayers.

9 x 12, 32 pp, HC, Full-color illus., ISBN 1-58023-080-6 **$16.95**

For Heaven's Sake

> For ages 4 & up

by *Sandy Eisenberg Sasso*; Full-color illus. by *Kathryn Kunz Finney*

Everyone talked about heaven: "Thank heavens." "Heaven forbid." "For heaven's sake, Isaiah." But no one would say what heaven was or how to find it. So Isaiah decides to find out, by seeking answers from many different people. "This book is a reminder of how well Sandy Sasso knows the minds of children. But it may surprise—and delight—readers to find how well she knows us grown-ups too." —Maria Harris, National Consultant in Religious Education, and author of *Teaching and Religious Imagination*
9 x 12, 32 pp, HC, Full-color illus., ISBN 1-58023-054-7 **$16.95**

But God Remembered
Stories of Women from Creation to the Promised Land

> For ages 8 & up

by *Sandy Eisenberg Sasso*; Full-color illus. by *Bethanne Andersen*

A fascinating collection of four different stories of women only briefly mentioned in biblical tradition and religious texts. Award-winning author Sasso vibrantly brings to life courageous and strong women from ancient tradition; all teach important values through their actions and faith. "Exquisite.... A book of beauty, strength and spirituality." —Association of Bible Teachers 9 x 12, 32 pp, HC, Full-color illus., ISBN 1-879045-43-5 **$16.95**

God in Between

> For ages 4 & up

by *Sandy Eisenberg Sasso*; Full-color illus. by *Sally Sweetland*

If you wanted to find God, where would you look? A magical, mythical tale that teaches that God can be found where we are: within all of us and the relationships between us. "This happy and wondrous book takes our children on a sweet and holy journey into God's presence." —Rabbi Wayne Dosick, Ph.D., author of *The Business Bible* and *Soul Judaism*
9 x 12, 32 pp, HC, Full-color illus., ISBN 1-879045-86-9 **$16.95**

Children's Spirituality

Because Nothing Looks Like God

by *Lawrence and Karen Kushner*
Full-color illus. by
Dawn W. Majewski

For ages 4 & up

MULTICULTURAL, NONDENOMINATIONAL, NONSECTARIAN

Real-life examples of happiness and sadness—from goodnight stories, to the hope and fear felt the first time at bat, to the closing moments of life—introduce children to the possibilities of spiritual life. A vibrant way for children—and their adults—to explore what, where, and how God is in our lives.

11 x 8½, 32 pp, HC, Full-color illus., ISBN 1-58023-092-X **$16.95**

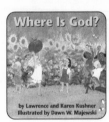 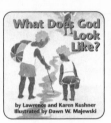  

Where Is God? (A Board Book)

For ages 0–4

by *Lawrence and Karen Kushner*; Full-color illus. by *Dawn W. Majewski*

A gentle way for young children to explore how God is with us every day, in every way. Abridged from *Because Nothing Looks Like God* by Lawrence and Karen Kushner and specially adapted to board book format to delight and inspire young readers.
5 x 5, 24 pp, Board, Full-color illus., ISBN 1-893361-17-9 **$7.95**

What Does God Look Like? (A Board Book)

For ages 0–4

by *Lawrence and Karen Kushner*; Full-color illus. by *Dawn W. Majewski*

A simple way for young children to explore the ways that we "see" God. Abridged from *Because Nothing Looks Like God* by Lawrence and Karen Kushner and specially adapted to board book format to delight and inspire young readers.
5 x 5, 24 pp, Board, Full-color illus., ISBN 1-893361-23-3 **$7.95**

How Does God Make Things Happen? (A Board Book)

For ages 0–4

by *Lawrence and Karen Kushner*; Full-color illus. by *Dawn W. Majewski*

A charming invitation for young children to explore how God makes things happen in our world. Abridged from *Because Nothing Looks Like God* by Lawrence and Karen Kushner and specially adapted to board book format to delight and inspire young readers.
5 x 5, 24 pp, Board, Full-color illus., ISBN 1-893361-24-1 **$7.95**

What Is God's Name? (A Board Book)

For ages 0–4

by *Sandy Eisenberg Sasso*; Full-color illus. by *Phoebe Stone*

Everyone and everything in the world has a name. What is God's name? Abridged from the award-winning *In God's Name* by Sandy Eisenberg Sasso and specially adapted to board book format to delight and inspire young readers.
5 x 5, 24 pp, Board, Full-color illus., ISBN 1-893361-10-1 **$7.95**

Children's Spirituality

Ten Amazing People
And How They Changed the World

For ages 6–10

by *Maura D. Shaw*; Foreword by *Dr. Robert Coles*
Full-color illus. by *Stephen Marchesi*

Black Elk • Dorothy Day • Malcolm X • Mahatma Gandhi •
Martin Luther King, Jr. • Mother Teresa • Janusz Korczak •
Desmond Tutu • Thich Nhat Hanh • Albert Schweitzer

This vivid, inspirational, and authoritative book will open new possibilities for children by telling the stories of how ten of the past century's greatest leaders changed the world in important ways.

8½, x 11, 48 pp, HC, Full-color illus., ISBN 1-893361-47-0 **$17.95**

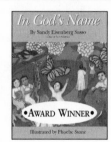

God's Paintbrush

For ages 4 & up

by *Sandy Eisenberg Sasso*; Full-color illus. by *Annette Compton*

Invites children of all faiths and backgrounds to encounter God openly in their own lives. Wonderfully interactive; provides questions adult and child can explore together at the end of each episode. "An excellent way to honor the imaginative breadth and depth of the spiritual life of the young." —Dr. Robert Coles, Harvard University
11 x 8½, 32 pp, HC, Full-color illus., ISBN 1-879045-22-2 **$16.95**

Also available:
A Teacher's Guide 8½ x 11, 32 pp, PB, ISBN 1-879045-57-5 **$8.95**
God's Paintbrush Celebration Kit 9½ x 12, HC, Includes 5 sessions/40 full-color Activity Sheets and Teacher Folder with complete instructions, ISBN 1-58023-050-4 **$21.95**

In God's Name

For ages 4 & up

by *Sandy Eisenberg Sasso*; Full-color illus. by *Phoebe Stone*

Like an ancient myth in its poetic text and vibrant illustrations, this award-winning modern fable about the search for God's name celebrates the diversity and, at the same time, the unity of all the people of the world. "What a lovely, healing book!" —Madeleine L'Engle
9 x 12, 32 pp, HC, Full-color illus., ISBN 1-879045-26-5 **$16.95**

Also available in Spanish:
El nombre de Dios 9 x 12, 32 pp, HC, Full-color illus., ISBN 1-893361-63-2 **$16.95**

Where Does God Live?

For ages 3–6

by *August Gold* and *Matthew J. Perlman*

Using simple, everyday examples that children can relate to, this colorful book helps young readers develop a personal understanding of God.
10 x 8½, 32 pp, Quality PB, Full-color photo illus., ISBN 1-893361-39-X **$7.95**

Religious Etiquette/Reference

How to Be a Perfect Stranger, 3rd Edition
The Essential Religious Etiquette Handbook
Edited by *Stuart M. Matlins* and *Arthur J. Magida*

The indispensable guidebook to help the well-meaning guest when visiting other people's religious ceremonies.

A straightforward guide to the rituals and celebrations of the major religions and denominations in the United States and Canada from the perspective of an interested guest of any other faith, based on information obtained from authorities of each religion. **Belongs in every living room, library, and office.**

COVERS:

African American Methodist Churches • Assemblies of God • Baha'i • Baptist • Buddhist • Christian Church (Disciples of Christ) • Christian Science (Church of Christ, Scientist) • Churches of Christ • Episcopalian and Anglican • Hindu • Islam • Jehovah's Witnesses • Jewish • Lutheran • Mennonite/Amish • Methodist • Mormon (Church of Jesus Christ of Latter-day Saints) • Native American/First Nations • Orthodox Churches • Pentecostal Church of God • Presbyterian • Quaker (Religious Society of Friends) • Reformed Church in America/Canada • Roman Catholic • Seventh-day Adventist • Sikh • Unitarian Universalist • United Church of Canada • United Church of Christ

6 x 9, 432 pp, Quality PB, ISBN 1-893361-67-5 **$19.95**

Also available:

The Perfect Stranger's Guide to Funerals and Grieving Practices
A Guide to Etiquette in Other People's Religious Ceremonies
Edited by *Stuart M. Matlins*
6 x 9, 240 pp, Quality PB, ISBN 1-893361-20-9 **$16.95**

The Perfect Stranger's Guide to Wedding Ceremonies
A Guide to Etiquette in Other People's Religious Ceremonies
Edited by *Stuart M. Matlins*
6 x 9, 208 pp, Quality PB, ISBN 1-893361-19-5 **$16.95**

Spirituality

Journeys of Simplicity
Traveling Light with Thomas Merton, Bashō, Edward Abbey, Annie Dillard & Others
by *Philip Harnden*

There is a more graceful way of traveling through life.

Offers vignettes of forty "travelers" and the few ordinary things they carried with them—from place to place, from day to day, from birth to death. What Thoreau took to Walden Pond. What Thomas Merton packed for his final trip to Asia. What Annie Dillard keeps in her writing tent. What an impoverished cook served M. F. K. Fisher for dinner. Much more.

"'How much should I carry with me?' is the quintessential question for any journey, especially the journey of life. Herein you'll find sage, sly, wonderfully subversive advice."
—Bill McKibben, author of *The End of Nature* and *Enough*
5 x 7¼, 128 pp, HC, ISBN 1-893361-76-4 **$16.95**

The Alphabet of Paradise
An A–Z of Spirituality for Everyday Life
by *Howard Cooper*

One of the most eloquent new voices in spirituality, Howard Cooper takes us on a journey of discovery—into ourselves and into the past—to find the signposts that can help us live more meaningful lives. In twenty-six engaging chapters—from A to Z—Cooper spiritually illuminates the subjects of daily life, using an ancient Jewish mystical method of interpretation that reveals both the literal and more allusive meanings of each. Topics include: Awe, Bodies, Creativity, Dreams, Emotions, Sports, and more.
6 x 9, 224 pp, Quality PB, ISBN 1-893361-80-2 **$16.95**

Winter
A Spiritual Biography of the Season
Edited by *Gary Schmidt* and *Susan M. Felch*; Illustrations by *Barry Moser*

Explore how the dormancy of winter can be a time of spiritual preparation and transformation.

In thirty stirring pieces, *Winter* delves into the varied feelings that winter conjures in us, calling up both the barrenness and the beauty of the natural world in wintertime. Includes selections by Will Campbell, Rachel Carson, Annie Dillard, Donald Hall, Ron Hansen, Jane Kenyon, Jamaica Kincaid, Barry Lopez, Kathleen Norris, John Updike, E. B. White, and many others.

"This outstanding anthology features top-flight nature and spirituality writers on the fierce, inexorable season of winter.... Remarkably lively and warm, despite the icy subject."
—★*Publishers Weekly* Starred Review
6 x 9, 288 pp, 6 b/w illus., HC, ISBN 1-893361-53-5 **$21.95**

Other Interesting Books—Spirituality

White Fire: A Portrait of Women Spiritual Leaders in America
by *Malka Drucker*; Photographs by *Gay Block*

This remarkable book gives voice and image to the often ignored, invisible, or overlooked narrative of women's spiritual leadership in America today. Includes insightful interviews and photographs of thirty-one female spiritual leaders, including Sylvia Boorstein, Beatrice Bruteau, Debbie Friedman, Leontine Kelly, Elaine Pagels, Iyanla Vanzant, Marianne Williamson, and many more. 7 x 10, 320 pp, HC, b/w photos, ISBN 1-893361-64-0 **$24.95**

Releasing the Creative Spirit: Unleash the Creativity in Your Life
by *Dan Wakefield*

From the author of *How Do We Know When It's God?*— a practical guide to accessing creative power in every area of your life.

Explodes the myths associated with the creative process and shows how everyone can uncover and develop their natural ability to create. Drawing on religion, psychology, and the arts, Dan Wakefield teaches us that the key to creation of any kind is clarity—of body, mind, and spirit—and he provides practical exercises that each of us can do to access that centered quality that allows creativity to shine. 7 x 10, 256 pp, Quality PB, ISBN 1-893361-36-5 **$16.95**

Spiritual Innovators: Seventy-Five Extraordinary People Who Changed the World in the Past Century
Edited by *Ira Rifkin* and *the Editors at SkyLight Paths*; Foreword by *Robert Coles*

Black Elk, H. H. the Dalai Lama, Abraham Joshua Heschel, Martin Luther King, Jr., Krishnamurti, C. S. Lewis, Aimee Semple McPherson, Thomas Merton, Elijah Muhammad, Simone Weil, and many more.

Profiles of the most important spiritual leaders of the past one hundred years. An invaluable reference of twentieth-century religion and an inspiring resource for spiritual challenge today. Authoritative list of seventy-five includes mystics and martyrs, intellectuals and charismatics from the East and West. For each, includes a brief biography, inspiring quotes and resources for more in-depth study.
6 x 9, 304 pp, b/w photographs, Quality PB, ISBN 1-893361-50-0 **$16.95**; HC, ISBN 1-893361-43-8 **$24.95**

Or phone, fax, mail or e-mail to: SKYLIGHT PATHS Publishing
Sunset Farm Offices, Route 4 • P.O. Box 237 • Woodstock, Vermont 05091
Tel: (802) 457-4000 • Fax: (802) 457-4004 • www.skylightpaths.com
Credit card orders: (800) 962-4544 (8:30AM–5:30PM ET Monday–Friday)
Generous discounts on quantity orders. SATISFACTION GUARANTEED. Prices subject to change.